The Weird Wide Web

The Weird Wide Web

Erfert Fenton and David Pogue

IDG Books Worldwide, Inc.
An International Data Group Company

Foster City, CA ✳ Chicago, IL ✳ Indianapolis, IN ✳ Southlake, TX

The Weird Wide Web

Published by
IDG Books Worldwide, Inc.
An International Data Group Company
919 E. Hillsdale Blvd., Suite 400
Foster City, CA 94404
http://www.idgbooks.com (IDG Books Worldwide Web site)

Cover photo credit: Photo of "The Nut Lady" courtesy of The Roadside America Project

Library of Congress Catalog Card No.: 97-70940

ISBN: 1-7645-4004-1

Printed in the United States of America

10 9 8 7 6 5 4 3 2

1IPC/RX/QU/ZX/FC

Distributed in the United States by IDG Books Worldwide, Inc.

Distributed by Macmillan Canada for Canada; by Contemporanea de Ediciones for Venezuela; by Distribuidora Cuspide for Argentina; by CITEC for Brazil; by Ediciones ZETA S.C.R. Ltda. for Peru; by Editorial Limusa SA for Mexico; by Transworld Publishers Limited in the United Kingdom and Europe; by Academic Bookshop for Egypt; by Levant Distributors S.A.R.L. for Lebanon; by Al Jassim for Saudi Arabia; by Simron Pty. Ltd. for South Africa; by Pustak Mahal for India; by The Computer Bookshop for India; by Toppan Company Ltd. for Japan; by Addison Wesley Publishing Company for Korea; by Longman Singapore Publishers Ltd. for Singapore, Malaysia, Thailand, and Indonesia; by Unalis Corporation for Taiwan; by WS Computer Publishing Company, Inc. for the Philippines; by WoodsLane Pty. Ltd. for Australia; by WoodsLane Enterprises Ltd. for New Zealand. Authorized Sales Agent: Anthony Rudkin Associates for the Middle East and North Africa.

For general information on IDG Books Worldwide's books in the U.S., please call our Consumer Customer Service department at 800-762-2974. For reseller information, including discounts and premium sales, please call our Reseller Customer Service department at 800-434-3422.

For information on where to purchase IDG Books Worldwide's books outside the U.S., please contact our International Sales department at 415-655-3023 or fax 415-655-3299.

For information on foreign language translations, please contact our Foreign and Subsidiary Rights department at 415-655-3021 or fax 415-655-3281.

For sales inquiries and special prices for bulk quantities, please contact our Sales department at 415-655-3200 or write to the address above.

For information on using IDG Books Worldwide's books in the classroom or for ordering examination copies, please contact our Educational Sales department at 800-434-2086 or fax 817-251-8174.

For press review copies, author interviews, or other publicity information, please contact our Public Relations department at 415-655-3000 or fax 415-655-3299.

For authorization to photocopy items for corporate, personal, or educational use, please contact Copyright Clearance Center, 222 Rosewood Drive, Danvers, MA 01923, or fax 508-750-4470.

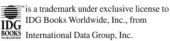

™ is a trademark under exclusive license to
IDG IDG Books Worldwide, Inc., from
BOOKS International Data Group, Inc.

1/29/97

ABOUT IDG BOOKS WORLDWIDE

Welcome to the world of IDG Books Worldwide.

IDG Books Worldwide, Inc., is a subsidiary of International Data Group, the world's largest publisher of computer-related information and the leading global provider of information services on information technology. IDG was founded more than 25 years ago and now employs more than 8,500 people worldwide. IDG publishes more than 275 computer publications in over 75 countries (see listing below). More than 60 million people read one or more IDG publications each month.

Launched in 1990, IDG Books Worldwide is today the #1 publisher of best-selling computer books in the United States. We are proud to have received eight awards from the Computer Press Association in recognition of editorial excellence and three from *Computer Currents'* First Annual Readers' Choice Awards. Our best-selling *...For Dummies*® series has more than 30 million copies in print with translations in 30 languages. IDG Books Worldwide, through a joint venture with IDG's Hi-Tech Beijing, became the first U.S. publisher to publish a computer book in the People's Republic of China. In record time, IDG Books Worldwide has become the first choice for millions of readers around the world who want to learn how to better manage their businesses.

Our mission is simple: Every one of our books is designed to bring extra value and skill-building instructions to the reader. Our books are written by experts who understand and care about our readers. The knowledge base of our editorial staff comes from years of experience in publishing, education, and journalism — experience we use to produce books for the '90s. In short, we care about books, so we attract the best people. We devote special attention to details such as audience, interior design, use of icons, and illustrations. And because we use an efficient process of authoring, editing, and desktop publishing our books electronically, we can spend more time ensuring superior content and spend less time on the technicalities of making books.

You can count on our commitment to deliver high-quality books at competitive prices on topics you want to read about. At IDG Books Worldwide, we continue in the IDG tradition of delivering quality for more than 25 years. You'll find no better book on a subject than one from IDG Books Worldwide.

John Kilcullen
CEO
IDG Books Worldwide, Inc.

Steven Berkowitz
President and Publisher
IDG Books Worldwide, Inc.

Eighth Annual Computer Press Awards ≥1992

Ninth Annual Computer Press Awards ≥1993

Tenth Annual Computer Press Awards ≥1994

Eleventh Annual Computer Press Awards ≥1995

IDG Books Worldwide, Inc., is a subsidiary of International Data Group, the world's largest publisher of computer-related information and the leading global provider of information services on information technology. International Data Group publishes over 275 computer publications in over 75 countries. Sixty million people read one or more International Data Group publications each month. International Data Group's publications include: **ARGENTINA:** Buyer's Guide, Computerworld Argentina, PC World Argentina; **AUSTRALIA:** Australian Macworld, Australian PC World, Australian Reseller News, Computerworld, IT Casebook, Network World, Publish, Webmaster; **AUSTRIA:** Computerwelt Osterreich, Networks Austria, PC Tip Austria; **BANGLADESH:** PC World Bangladesh; **BELARUS:** PC World Belarus; **BELGIUM:** Data News; **BRAZIL:** Annuário de Informática, Computerworld, Connections, Macworld, PC Player, PC World, Publish, Reseller News, Supergamepower; **BULGARIA:** Computerworld Bulgaria, Network World Bulgaria, PC & MacWorld Bulgaria; **CANADA:** CIO Canada, Client/Server World, ComputerWorld Canada, InfoWorld Canada, NetworkWorld Canada, WebWorld; **CHILE:** Computerworld Chile, PC World Chile; **COLOMBIA:** Computerworld Colombia, PC World Colombia; **COSTA RICA:** PC World Centro America; **THE CZECH AND SLOVAK REPUBLICS:** Computerworld Czechoslovakia, Macworld Czech Republic, PC World Czechoslovakia; **DENMARK:** Communications World Danmark, Computerworld Danmark, Macworld Danmark, PC World Danmark, Techworld Denmark; **DOMINICAN REPUBLIC:** PC World Republica Dominicana; **ECUADOR:** PC World Ecuador; **EGYPT:** Computerworld Middle East, PC World Middle East; **EL SALVADOR:** PC World Centro America; **FINLAND:** MikroPC, Tietoverkko, Tietoviikko; **FRANCE:** Distributique, Hebdo, Info PC, Le Monde Informatique, Macworld, Reseaux & Telecoms, WebMaster France; **GERMANY:** Computer Partner, Computerwoche, Computerwoche Extra, Computerwoche FOCUS, Global Online, Macwelt, PC Welt; **GREECE:** Amiga Computing, GamePro Greece, Multimedia World; **GUATEMALA:** PC World Centro America; **HONDURAS:** PC World Centro America; **HONG KONG:** Computerworld Hong Kong, PC World Hong Kong, Publish in Asia; **HUNGARY:** ABCD CD-ROM, Computerworld Szamitastechnika, Internetto online Magazine, PC World Hungary, PC-X Magazin Hungary; **ICELAND:** Tolvuheimur PC World Island; **INDIA:** Information Communications World, Information Systems Computerworld, PC World India, Publish in Asia; **INDONESIA:** InfoKomputer PC World, Komputek Computerworld, Publish in Asia; **IRELAND:** ComputerScope, PC Live!; **ISRAEL:** Macworld Israel, People & Computers/Computerworld; **ITALY:** Computerworld Italia, Macworld Italia, Networking Italia, PC World Italia; **JAPAN:** DTP World, Macworld Japan, Nikkei Personal Computing, OS/2 World Japan, SunWorld Japan, Windows NT World, Windows World Japan; **KENYA:** PC World East African; **KOREA:** Hi-Tech Information, Macworld Korea, PC World Korea; **MACEDONIA:** PC World Macedonia; **MALAYSIA:** Computerworld Malaysia, PC World Malaysia, Publish in Asia; **MALTA:** PC World Malta; **MEXICO:** Computerworld Mexico, PC World Mexico, **MYANMAR:** PC World Myanmar; **NETHERLANDS:** Computer! Totaal, LAN Internetworking Magazine, LAN World Buyers Guide, Macworld Netherlands, Net, WebWereld; **NEW ZEALAND:** Absolute Beginners Guide and Plain & Simple Series, Computer Buyer, Computer Industry Directory, Computerworld New Zealand, MTB, Network World, PC World New Zealand; **NICARAGUA:** PC World Centro America; **NORWAY:** Computerworld Norge, CW Rapport, Datamagasinet, Financial Rapport, Kursguide Norge, Macworld Norge, Multimediaworld Norge, PC World Nettverk, PC World Norge, PC World ProduktGuide Norge; **PAKISTAN:** Computerworld Pakistan; **PANAMA:** PC World Panama; **PEOPLE'S REPUBLIC OF CHINA:** China Computer Users, China Computerworld, China InfoWorld, China Telecom World Weekly, Computer & Communication, Electronic Design China, Electronics Today, Electronics Weekly, Game Software, PC World China, Popular Computer Week, Software Weekly, Software World, Telecom World; **PERU:** Computerworld Peru, PC World Profesional Peru, PC World SoHo Peru; **PHILIPPINES:** Click!, Computerworld Philippines, PC World Philippines, Publish in Asia; **POLAND:** Computerworld Poland, Computerworld Special Report Poland, Cyber, Macworld Poland, Networld Poland, PC World Komputer; **PORTUGAL:** Cerebro/PC World, Computerworld/Correio Informático, Dealer World Portugal, Mac*In/PC*In Portugal, Multimedia World; **PUERTO RICO:** PC World Puerto Rico; **ROMANIA:** Computerworld Romania, PC World Romania, Telecom Romania; **RUSSIA:** Computerworld Russia, Mir PK, Publish, Seti; **SINGAPORE:** Computerworld Singapore, PC World Singapore, Publish in Asia; **SLOVENIA:** Monitor; **SOUTH AFRICA:** Computing SA, Network World SA, Software World SA; **SPAIN:** Communicaciones World España, Computerworld España, Dealer World España, Macworld España, PC World España; **SRI LANKA:** Infolink PC World; **SWEDEN:** CAP&Design, Computer Sweden, Corporate Computing Sweden, Internetworld Sweden, it branschen, Macworld Sweden, MaxiData Sweden, MikroDatorn, Nätverk & Kommunikation, PC World Sweden, PCAktiv, Windows World Sweden; **SWITZERLAND:** Computerworld Schweiz, Macworld Schweiz, PCtip; **TAIWAN:** Computerworld Taiwan, Macworld Taiwan, NEW ViSiON/Publish, PC World Taiwan, Windows World Taiwan; **THAILAND:** Publish in Asia, Thai Computerworld; **TURKEY:** Computerworld Turkiye, Macworld Turkiye, Network World Turkiye, PC World Turkiye; **UKRAINE:** Computerworld Kiev, Multimedia World Ukraine, PC World Ukraine; **UNITED KINGDOM:** Acorn User UK, Amiga Action UK, Amiga Computing UK, Apple Talk UK, Computing, Macworld, Parents and Computers UK, PC Advisor, PC Home, PSX Pro, The WEB; **UNITED STATES:** Cable in the Classroom, CIO Magazine, Computerworld, DOS World, Federal Computer Week, GamePro Magazine, InfoWorld, I-Way, Macworld, Network World, PC Games, PC World, Publish, Video Event, THE WEB Magazine, and WebMaster; online webzines: JavaWorld, NetscapeWorld, and SunWorld Online; **URUGUAY:** InfoWorld Uruguay; **VENEZUELA:** Computerworld Venezuela, PC World Venezuela; and **VIETNAM:** PC World Vietnam. 3/24/97

Credits

Acquisitions Editor
Nancy E. Dunn

Development Editor
Susan Pines

Technical Editor
Greg Guntle

Copy Editor
Larisa M. North

Production Coordinators
Phyllis Beaty
Ben Schroeter

Graphics and Production Specialist
Elsie Yim

Illustrator
Kurt Krames

Proofreader
Christine Langin-Faris

Indexer
Erfert Fenton

Book Designers
Margery Cantor
Kurt Krames

Cover Designer
Craig Hanson

Preface

When a team of U.S. Army scientists put together a vast, nationwide communications network called the Internet in the 1960s, their main concern was keeping information flowing—even if nuclear Armageddon struck. The Internet became a wonderful tool for scientists and academics, who exchanged ideas, published reports, conducted research, and participated in a glorious intellectual renaissance with their colleagues worldwide.

Then a catastrophe worse than nuclear Armageddon hit: the masses got hold of the thing. With the advent of the World Wide Web—and easy-to-use Web browsers that abolished those pesky UNIX commands that used to keep the rabble off the Internet—everybody suddenly *had* to be surfing the Web (even though they weren't quite sure why).

And as tools to create Web pages became widely available, every Joe with access to a computer felt compelled to publish his own home page, filled with excruciatingly detailed information on himself, his family, his hobbies, his pets, his favorite brand of dental floss, et cetera, *ad nauseam*. (We thought we'd throw in a little Latin there to impress you. It's the best we can do, *in lieu* of any academic credentials. Hey, look! We know some French, too!) In the blink of an eye, the quality of information on the Net went right down the toilet—sometimes, literally (see the infamous **Toiletcam** site described in Chapter 4).

That's not to say you can't still find useful information on the Web. *Au contraire*. If you look hard, you can find instructive sites such as **Watermelon: How to Remove All the Seeds** (http://www.best.com/~storm/me/melon/mellon1. htm), **How to Use Nose Drops** (http://www.pharm.su.oz.au/pwmirror/pwz/patient/ pharmwebpatinf6.html), **How to Burp a Baby** (http://www.learn2.com/04/0439/ 0439.html), and **How to Ride an Elevator Safely** (http://www.otis.com).

But overall, the Web seems to be slouching toward bedlam. Here are the results of a survey we took, using a software search engine to count the number of times certain words occurred on the Web:

✼ Scientific research
  "Nuclear fusion": 3,000
  "UFOs": 20,000

✼ Influential people
  "Madame Curie": 400
  "David Letterman": 10,000

- Music
  "Johann Sebastian Bach": 2,000
  "Metallica": 30,000
- Cuisine
  "Filet mignon": 3,000
  "Donuts": 10,000
- Agriculture
  "Chemical fertilizers": 1,000
  "Crop circles": 2,000

Need we say more?

As the Web's usefulness is plummeting, however, its level of fun is going through the roof. And that's what this book's about: The goofy, the witty, the off-color, and the generally weird pages that are wasting so much bandwidth—and receiving so many visitors—on the Web. We're talking UFO lore, vile experiments with Hostess Twinkies, poems about SPAM, and sound clips of William "Captain Kirk" Shatner "singing" "Lucy in the Sky with Diamonds."

We have painstakingly scoured the Web for what we think are the weirdest sites—but we can't cover them all. That would take a 30-volume encyclopedia. If you'd like to find still more weird Web sites, may we suggest two excellent resources: **Yahoo!'s Useless Pages Index** (http:// www.yahoo.com/Entertainment/Useless_Pages/) and the **Centre for the Easily Amused** (http://www.amused.com/).

Sadly (or happily, depending on your point of view), some of the sites described in this book will bite the dust sooner or later—some might even be gone by the time you read this. That's the nature of the Web. At least we can take some small comfort in the fact that these transitory wisps of code will be immortalized in these pages.

You don't have to know much about the World Wide Web to enjoy this book. If you have access to the Web, you can type in the URLs (the address gibberish that starts with "http://") for the sites we describe and visit them yourself. Or you can visit the **IDG Books Worldwide** Web page (http://www.idgbooks.com) and search for *The Weird Wide Web*. Open this book's Web page and then click the bonus content link for a list of links that will whisk you directly to the sites. And if you're one of the 12 or 13 people in the world who's not yet surfing the Web, don't worry—we think you'll still enjoy the book.

Why are there so many silly sites? We don't know. We don't pretend to be sociologists. (Well, OK, sometimes we do: "Honey, tonight let's pretend you're a lusty milkmaid and I'm a sociologist." But that's beside the point.)

Our task is merely to describe the strange sites we've seen and—we hope—make you laugh. But perhaps you won't laugh. Perhaps, as you see a Strawberry Pop-Tart burst into flames or read a debate on the alien autopsy film, you'll find yourself filled with a nameless horror as you watch Western Civilization crumble before your very eyes.

Lighten up. Civilization was already pretty far gone before the World Wide Web came into being; it just took the Web to get the word out. Our advice: laugh.

The World Wide Web today: "Oh! The inanity!"

A Weird Wide Web word of caution: Some of the Web sites described in this book include dangerous projects (launching Buicks with a catapult, for example, or inserting electrodes into dill pickles). Don't try these tricks at home. Really.

About the Authors

Erfert Fenton

Erfert Fenton is a ranch hand and technical writer who resides in California's fabled Silicon Valley. When she's not riding or writing, Erfert spends her time cruising the Web for bizarre sites, many of which have found their way into this book.

Erfert has been a Macworld magazine writer and editor since the Dawn of the Macintosh in 1984. Now that it's the Late Afternoon of the Macintosh, she's eyeing alternate careers, but hasn't come up with anything promising yet (except maybe trick roper). She's also the author of a number of computer books, including *The Macintosh Font Book* and *Art of Darkness: The After Dark Companion* (Peachpit Press).

Her e-mail address is erfert@fentonia.com. For years, she steadfastly refused to put up a home page on the Web, feeling — and justifiably so — that nobody really wants to know that she has three cats, is a student of Japanese flower arranging, and enjoys listening to old Roy Orbison records. After writing this book, however, she finally gave in; you can now visit her site at **http://www.fentonia.com/erf**.

David Pogue

Ohio-bred, Yale-educated, Connecticut resident David Pogue is the author of the #1 Mac bestseller *Macs For Dummies*, now in its fourth edition; its inevitable sequel, *MORE Macs For Dummies*; and *Macworld Mac FAQs*, the book of 500 frequently asked questions (and their answers).

He writes the back-page column, "The Desktop Critic," in Macworld. His novel, *Hard Drive* (Berkley Publishing Group), was called "a notable book of the year" by the New York Times. His Mac students include Stephen Sondheim, Carly Simon, Mike Nichols, Harry Connick, Jr., Gary Oldman, Natasha Richardson, and Mia Farrow.

In his other lives, David is a dinner-table magician, occasional Broadway conductor, and, with collaborator Joseph Schorr, composer of little-known musicals such as *Downtown Local* and *Odysseus: The Man and His Music*. His e-mail address is Pogue@aol.com and his weird Web page is at **http://www.concentric.net/~Pogue**.

Contents

Greetings from
The Weird Wide Web

Fun with Food

For some reason, people on the Web feel compelled to run diabolical experiments on food. And for some reason (probably the same one), we feel obliged to write about these experiments. Perhaps you'll come up with your own theories as to why these folks—and the countless visitors to their sites—find food experiments so fascinating. If nothing else, this chapter provides some food for thought—if you're on a strict intellectual diet.

So, what happens when you run a 110V AC current through a Hostess Twinkie? How about when you insert a Kellogg's Strawberry Pop-Tart in a toaster and hold the lever down? What do grapes do when subjected to microwaves? Are pickles a reliable source of illumination? Read on, and you'll learn the answers to these and other burning culinary questions.

SPAM: A Many-Splendored Lunch Meat

When sociologists ponder the nuances of Internet culture, they ultimately find themselves returning, again and again, to the same question: Why are there so many Web pages devoted to SPAM? Is Hormel's canned meat product perhaps a metaphor for the Internet itself—made up of diverse elements, ubiquitous, and virtually indestructible? Perhaps. Or perhaps that's a lot of intellectual baloney; maybe people just like writing about SPAM. Let's take a look at a few key SPAM sites to see if we can understand this odd phenomenon.

Any serious SPAMophile will want to start with Bob Gorman's **Page O' Spam** (http://semantic.rsi.com/spam/), which is the quintessential SPAM site—the SPAM de la SPAM. Here, you'll find links to the most important SPAM pages, including a history of SPAM, the **Find-the-Spam** game (http://www.smalltime.com/nowhere/findthespam/), the text of Monty Python's renowned SPAM skit, SPAM-related products, and even the Hormel Institute's home page. We approached the Spam Audio link with some trepidation, expecting recordings of the squishy "glorp" sound SPAM makes when liberated from its tin; happily, this page was composed of snippets from the aforementioned Monty Python routine, plus a musical tribute called "The Morning SPAM Song."

Can you find the SPAM?
© smalltime industries

Let's review a little SPAM history. The famous canned luncheon meat was developed in the 1930s by Jay C. Hormel, son of Hormel founder George A. Hormel. Lunchmeat scholars disagree as to whether the product's name derives from "spiced pork and ham" or "shoulder of pork and ham." Either way, the fact that it requires no refrigeration made SPAM a mainstay for troops during World War II. We're not quite sure how it became so popular with civilians, who didn't have to eat it, but somehow SPAM made its way to every supermarket in America. Not content to rest on their laurels, the folks at Hormel have introduced various SPAM spin-offs over the years, including—for health-conscious gourmands—reduced-salt/sodium SPAM and SPAM Lite.

Today, science marches on at **The Hormel Institute** (http://wolf.co.net/hi/), which was established in 1942 by the Regents of the University of Minnesota and the Hormel Foundation. "It is the mission of the Hormel Institute to conduct research and education in the biological sciences with applications in medicine and agriculture."

That's a lofty goal, but just exactly what are these guys up to? So far, only a single Hormel Institute researcher, one **Vitthal Shriniwas Kulkarni** (http://wolf.co.net/hi/personal/vsk/index.html) has put up a home page, but his current research projects should shed some light on the Hormel Institute's mission. At present, Dr. Kulkarni is "investigating thermotropic phase behavior of various *N*-acylated galactosylsphingosines, phospholipids and their mixtures with cholesterol. . . . Bilayer nanotubes and helical ribbons are discovered to be the exclusive microstructures in the aqueous dispersions of certain chain-specific glycosphingolipids." We're not positive, but we think that what he's doing, in layman's terms, is placing a slice of SPAM on a sunny windowsill and observing what happens to it. (On the other hand, maybe it's more serious. We don't want to alarm anyone, but according to Dr. Kulkarni's résumé, his previous research involved neurotoxins.)

If you have a thirst for knowledge but are intimidated by words with more than three syllables (er, that is, *scared* by words with more than three syllables), don't despair: there's a SPAM site just for you. The **Spam Cam** site (http://www.fright.com/cgi-bin/spamcam) attempts to answer the question, "How does Spam decompose compared to other organic materials?"

The intrepid researchers at this site have aimed a camera at a plate of SPAM and several control foods: a tomato, some green Jell-O, and a Twinkie, for example. The test objects reside in a kitchen where the average ambient temperature is 68 degrees Fahrenheit. Every few days an updated photo is shown, illustrating the progress of the items' decay. (Warning to sensitive readers: this is not a pretty site!) From this experiment we can conclude two things:

✺ SPAM does, indeed, eventually begin to rot when removed from its protective can and left at room temperature.

✺ These researchers do not live with their mother.

The following illustrations and lab notes show the progress of one experiment.

Lab notes from 2/02/96: "Based on feedback from our many Spam Cam visitors, we are now comparing SPAM to a Twinkie, a tomato, and Jell-O. We will attempt to compare and contrast the rates of decay among these select items. And praise be, we've already learned something significant: it takes a long time for Jell-O to set. (Bill Cosby never said anything about set time.) We're also investigating the possible sentience of the subjects. No, we're not stupid enough to think that Jell-O has a mind, but what about the SPAM and the tomato?"

[Editor's note: Hey! What about the Twinkies? The researchers at The T.W.I.N.K.I.E.S. Project, which is described later in this chapter, attempt to ascertain whether Twinkies possess intelligence.]

Experiment #2: 2/02/96

Lab notes from 2/15/96: "Violence befalls us! In the quiet of late last evening, the dying tomato caved into itself, spewing its innards at the hapless Twinkies. Now soaked in tomato rot (A), we can only assume that the Twinkies' preservative armor has been compromised. Alas, Twinkie death is sure to follow. On a lighter note, the SPAM's distinctive mold circles (B) are sprouting thousands of tiny hairs. This could represent yet another Spam Cam pharmacological breakthrough . . . could rotting SPAM be the ultimate cure for male pattern baldness? SPAM researchers are contacting the Hair Club for Men to solicit volunteers."

Experiment #2: 2/15/96

Lab notes from 3/3/96: "The end is near. The time has come to end experiment 2. The Jell-O jigglers are slick with white ooze (A), the SPAM is an unresponsive hairy blob (C), the Twinkies are soggy with tomato juice mold (B), and the resultant stench is sturdy enough to don a physical body. (Some researchers are convinced that the tomato's white goiter is actually the odor's developing head.) We won't continue monitoring the current experiment (as we've been doing with our first project) because we can't get anyone to get close enough to photograph the subjects. Our next project will be arranged to insure that intrasubject contamination does not take place, hopefully minimizing odor problems."

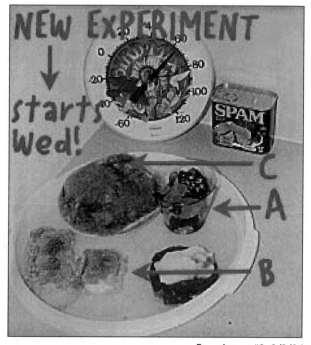

Experiment #2: 3/3/96

So far, we've been concentrating on the scientific aspects of SPAM. But we must not neglect SPAM's contribution to the Humanities—namely, the **SPAM Haiku Archive** (http://www.naic.edu/~jcho/spam/sha.html). To be accurate, it should be noted that many of the verses here are closer to senryu. Haiku is a verse form about nature with a seasonal reference, traditionally written in a 5-7-5 syllable pattern. Senryu are haiku-like verse forms, but are not necessarily about nature (which is good, beacuse SPAM is definitely not found in nature). The archive contains more than 6,000 SPAM poems, and you are invited to contribute your own. Here are some noteworthy examples:

Supermarket aisle.
Mom pushes cart toward SPAM shelf.
Child bursts into tears.
— © John Nagamichi Cho

Someone please tell me
Do they have to starve the pigs
When making SPAM LITE?
— Tom Elliott

Worse than eating SPAM?
Watching your father-in-law
eat a trout head. (Crunch.)
— Matt Ragozzin

Descartes on pig parts
Says: "I'm pink, therefore I'm SPAM"
Deep philosophy
— Chris Fishel

The Web features many other SPAM-related pages, but these pages are beyond the scope of this book. [Editor's note: That phrase, which you will find in almost every technical book, really means that an author is too lazy to write about something.] A little-known use for SPAM involves actually eating it, but for humanitarian reasons we will spare you the links to SPAM recipes, which include such treats as Deviled Green Eggs and SPAM, SPAM Strudel, and SPAMsicles.

A SIDE OF SPAM

■ Say the word "SPAM" to a gourmet and he will curl his lip in distaste. Say the word "SPAM" to an Internet user and he will start frothing at the mouth and launch into a tirade. That's because, in the Internet world, "spamming" refers to the unsavory practice of sending out mass quantities of unsolicited e-mail. The term is said to have been inspired by the famous Monty Python sketch in which a restaurant offers SPAM, SPAM, SPAM, SPAM, and SPAM. (For the text of the **Monty Python SPAM Sketch,** see http://www.rsi.com/spam/ spam-skit.html).

The most infamous spammers of them all are Laurence Canter and Martha Siegel, husband-and-wife partners in the immigration law firm of Canter and Siegel. (For an excellent collec-tion of lawyer jokes, see **Nolo's Favorite Lawyer Jokes** at http:// www.nolo.com /jokes/jokes.html. But we digress.) In April of 1994, Canter and Siegel provoked the wrath of the Internet community when they posted an advertisement offering their services on thousands of Usenet newsgroups. A flood of messages from angry recipients caused the computer at Canter & Siegel's Internet service provider to crash, and spamming has been a lively topic of discussion in Internet circles ever since. Spamming brings up issues of personal privacy, freedom of speech, and the commercial viability of the Net. From the perspective of this book, e-mail SPAM adds thousands of unwanted references when one wants to do an online search for the canned meat product. ■

Tortured Twinkies and Charred Pop-Tarts

If you were impressed by the scientific zeal shown by the Spam Cam researchers, wait until you see **The T.W.I.N.K.I.E.S. Project** (http://www.owlnet. rice.edu/~gouge/twinkies.html).

T.W.I.N.K.I.E.S., in case you were wondering, stands for Tests With Inorganic Noxious Kakes In Extreme Situations.

At this site, researchers Chris Gouge and Todd Stadler perform a number of educational experiments on Hostess Twinkies. Their methodology is praiseworthy; for example, each experiment involves a control Twinkie in addition to the test Twinkie to ensure scientific validity. Unfortunately, a few of the control subjects were eaten by bystanders, compromising some of the results.

The indefatigable Gouge and Stadler subject Twinkies to electricity, gravity, radiation, heat, liquids, and the "liquefy" cycle of a blender.

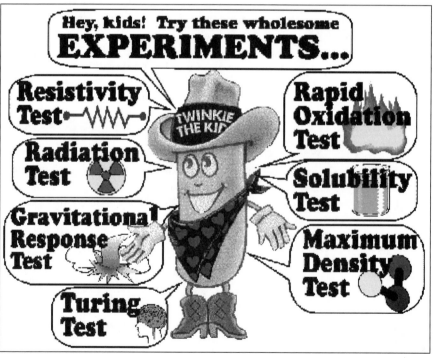

A battery of Twinkie tests

While skeptics might doubt the usefulness of these experiments, the researchers are careful to suggest real-world applications for their discoveries. For example, in the resistivity test, in which a 110V standard household current is passed through a Twinkie, Gouge and Stadler observed that almost no current passed through the test Twinkie. Possible applications: "If you want to electrically isolate a room from static or higher voltage electricity, you can simply line it with Twinkies. If a power line has fallen in the road and you want to move it, you simply wrap the line in Twinkies, and then it is safe for moving . . . the possibilities are endless!"

In the gravitational response test, in which a Twinkie was dropped from a six-story building—twice—with minimal damage, the researchers concluded that Twinkies maintain a good deal of structural integrity after such a fall. Possible applications: "If one needed to jump off of the sixth floor of [a building] and land safely, one could either pad the ground or one's self with Twinkies, which although they would not probably survive the fall, would break your fall so that you could escape unharmed. Note: We have not experimentally verified this application, and do not suggest you do so either. In the event you do not heed our warning, however, could you tell us how it went? Thanks."

In one groundbreaking experiment, Gouge and Stadler attempt to discern whether Twinkies possess intelligence. "This test was a slightly modified version of the Turing test, designed to check computers for artificial intellegence (sic)." [The reason that computers will eventually pass the Turing test and surpass humans in all intellectual tasks is that computers, unlike humans, can have built-in spelling checkers.] "The theory is that if you get responses from one human and one other thing (originally a computer program) without knowing which is which, and cannot determine from those responses which was given by the other object, then the other object must be at least as intelligent as a human."

After placing the human subject and the Twinkie behind a screen and asking each a series of questions, the researchers concluded that Twinkies do not, in fact, exhibit any intelligence. (They had some additional concerns as to whether their human subject exhibited any intelligence, but they gave him the benefit of the doubt.) This conclusion greatly assuaged the consciences of the researchers, considering the horrible things they had done to the test Twinkies.

Man versus Twinkie: The Turing test

By now the astute reader (that's right, there's only one—this book isn't exactly designed to attract brainiacs, now, is it?) will have noticed that The T.W.I.N.K.I.E.S. Project, by dint of its title (the astute reader will also know what "dint" means; we sure don't), postulates that Twinkies are inorganic. Whereas the Spam Cam scientists ("How does Spam decompose compared to other organic materials?") assume that Twinkies are organic. How do we explain this discrepancy? Needless to say, it's beyond the scope of this book. We can only issue a plea to the scientists in both camps to provide empirical data on the organic properties—if any—of Twinkies. The Web, after all, provides the ideal forum for the pursuit of Truth, the betterment of Mankind, and the gratuitous use of Capitalized Words.

While we're on the subject of culinary research, it's time to discuss another enlightening site: the **Strawberry Pop-Tart Blow-Torches** page (http://www.sci.tamucc.edu/%7Epmichaud/toast/). Yes, folks, it's a scientific fact that Strawberry Pop-Tarts, when left in a toaster for an extended period of time, will emit spectacular jets of flame. This phenomenon was recorded by humorist Dave Barry, and is scientifically verified on the Strawberry Pop-Tart Blow-Torches page. Researcher Patrick R. Michaud presents a well-documented experiment in which he places two Strawberry Pop-Tarts in a toaster, sets it to the darkest setting, tapes the lever down to prevent the Pop-Tarts from being ejected, and plugs in the toaster. (Dr. Michaud is no fool; he conducted the experiment in his driveway, using a long extension cord.)

The results, which are documented in photos and meticulous field notes, are impressive. Here's an excerpt: "... large amounts of smoke began pouring out of the toaster. The researchers noticed that some of the neighbors down the street were beginning to get a little curious, but the experiment proceeded nonetheless. Approximately 40 seconds later, small flames began licking their way out of the toaster. The flames steadily grew larger and larger until reaching a maximum height of about 18 inches above the top of the toaster."

Strawberry Pop-Tarts flambée

(For another researcher's work with Strawberry Pop-Tart Blow Torches, see Dr. Roger A. Hunt's **Flaming Pop-Tart Experiment** at http://www.personal.umich.edu/~gmbrown/tart/.)

Dr. Michaud's experiments involving thermal energy and foodstuffs are not confined to Pop-Tarts. In **Fun with Grapes — A Case Study** (http://www.sci.tamucc.edu/~pmichaud/grape/) he demonstrates that "Ordinary grapes, when properly prepared and microwaved, spark impressively in an extremely entertaining manner."

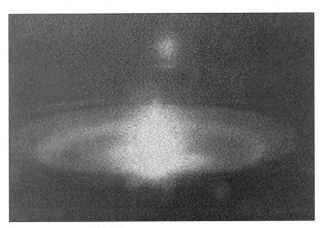

Liven up a grape with microwaves.

In this experiment, Dr. Michaud slices a grape in half, places it in a microwave oven, and produces some amazing pyrotechnics. (In the name of Scientific Accuracy—and/or in the name of Having Nothing Better to Do on a Wednesday Night—we tried this experiment at home. Conclusions: the pyrotechnics were spectacular, but the smell of burning grapeflesh was sickening.)

Pickles and Ice Cream and Liquefied Gases

Another impressive food-oriented science project can be found at http://www.research.digital.com/wrl/techreports/html/TN-13. **Characterization of Organic Illumination Systems** is a report of experiments performed by seven scientists at DEC's Western Research Laboratory that "presents a quantitative study of an organic illumination system, characterizing the temperature and current-flow properties of the system as functions of time and device parameters." In layman's terms: they make pickles light up by sticking electrodes in them.

A pickle, thanks to its high salt content, is an excellent conductor. As a result, after the water near the electrodes starts to boil, a bright arc of electricity shoots from one electrode to the other, causing a greenish glow.

To ensure thorough exploration of this potentially revolutionary discovery, the researchers test five different media—dill, kosher, and cornichon pickles (the latter "chosen for experimentation with miniaturization of this technology")—plus two non-pickle media: a mandarin orange slice and a piece of stir-fried bok choy. The results are—forgive us—illuminating. The pickles produced respectable arcs, the bok choy fizzled, and the mandarin orange segment "never really lit up." Graphs showing current and temperature over time are provided for each of the test media.

Noting that the paper was dated April 1, 1989, your present authors were somewhat skeptical of its authenticity. Therefore, in the interest of Not Really Having Anything to Do on Thursday Night Either, we invited some scientific colleagues over and proceeded to zap a pickle ourselves. The scientific results: the sucker lit up like a Christmas tree! (As we performed the experiment a few days before Christmas, we were able to verify this observation empirically.) Our first test pickle, a Vlasic kosher dill, lit up brightly for more than a minute, producing, in addition to a bright green glow, a loud crackling noise, yellow sparks, billowing smoke, and a vile stench. We were impressed. Subsequent test subjects involved a sweet pickle (a moderate glow), a piece of kim-chee—aka Korean pickled cabbage, for those readers who dine exclusively at Denny's—(a few flickers and an odor even worse than non-electrified kim-chee), and a tomato (total darkness).

The stalwart scientists at DEC are quick to point out the practical advantages of this surprising phenomenon. "The primary advantage of pickles as light bulbs is that they can be eaten, either before or after providing illumination. Thus they are to be preferred for long sea voyages." We admit we hadn't thought of that.

On the other hand, pickle bulbs may not yet be ready for prime time. For one thing, "the very small color range of organic illumination systems is a serious drawback . . . pickles limit us mainly to green." For another, "Arcing pickles smell bad, [which] may prove to severely limit opportunities for exploiting this technology commercially." [Authors' note: We'll vouch for that!]

Commercial applications of "dillumination"? We can just see it: "The new Vlasic 75-watt flood pickle. So bright it crunches."

We're guessing that the daredevil chefs we've described in this chapter find themselves in a nightly quandary. After destroying their toasters and microwaves by performing insane experiments on various foods, how can they cook tonight's dinner? Well, they might consider using their barbeque grills. But it takes so long for the coals to get ready!

Unless, of course, they light their charcoal briquettes with liquid oxygen instead of that wimpy lighter fluid. That's exactly how George H. Goble does it on his **Grill Lighting** page at http://ghg.ecn.purdue.edu/.

George Goble: A fun guy to invite to a picnic

Mr. Goble, a senior systems engineer in Purdue University's Electrical Engineering Department, has lit many a grill with liquid oxygen and provides photos, movies, and sound clips of his exploits. While traditional grill-lighting methods take half an hour to get the coals white-hot, Mr. Goble's technique heats up the grill in about 3 seconds. As a bonus, this method conveniently burns off any old grease and debris from the grill.

We have ignition.

A hearty "Well done"

On the negative side, it pretty much vaporizes the grill.

In addition to his enlightening text, photos, and movies, Mr. Goble's site provides some sound advice for would-be grill lighters: "Don't try this at home."

When it comes to using liquefied gases in cooking, however, there's more to gaseous temperature extremes than Mr. Goble's liquid oxygen. We refer, of course, to liquid *nitrogen*, which, because it's well under 200 degrees below zero, isn't much use on the grill. It occurred to the resourceful H. Henry Rieke IV, however, that liquid nitrogen has culinary potential — it's ideal, in fact, for making ice cream. He provides complete instructions for the home chemistry buff at what he calls "the first **Liquid Nitrogen Ice Cream** page on the Internet" (http:// 157.182.174.110/Henry/icecream.html), a claim we're fairly sure is accurate.

The ingredients are simple — milk, heavy cream, real vanilla ("not that fake junk!"), sugar, and liquid nitrogen — and are accompanied by photos, a video, and friendly reminders not to stick your bodily appendages into the superfreezing fluid. You don't even need an ice-cream machine or other special equipment for this recipe — just the standard mixing bowl, wooden spoon, and heavily insulated ski gloves found in any kitchen.

Butter (Not), Studmuffins, and Other Delights

Enough with the culinary science projects. Food, as you know, has traditionally been used for eating. The Web has its share of food-for-food's-sake sites as well.

As the saying goes, the way to a man's heart is through his stomach. (The path to a woman's heart is apparently uncharted, or if not, has yet to acquire a cute adage.) Therefore, gals, we urge you to make a beeline for the Romantic Recipes section of the **I Can't Believe It's Not Butter!** home page (http://www.tasteyoulove.com/index.html).

ICBINB! (pronounced *Ich bin Bee!*) is, as its name implies, an extremely butterlike substance that one can use in place of real-butter products (such as I Believe This Is Actually Butter!™) for applications such as cooking. In fact, ICBINB! must be a very popular cooking aid — our studies show that it's used in fully 100 percent of the recipes on the ICBINB! home page.

You'll no doubt be thrilled to see that Fabio, "The King of Romance," is featured on ICBINB!'s site. Those flowing yellow tresses, those smooth, sculpted pectoral muscles . . . we can't believe *he's* not butter! (Note: If this page doesn't provide enough Fabio for you, you can always visit the **Fabio** page at http://redwood.northcoast.com/~shojo/Fabio/fabio.html. Here you can click on sultry photos of the Shirtless One lounging by the pool, lounging on black satin sheets, lounging in the sauna, or lounging on the hood of a Rolls Royce [the latter involves Advanced Lounging Skills; it costs a fortune to get pectoral-shaped dents out of a Rolls] and hear him croon phrases such as "I have memories of our perfect time together." You wish.)

So, what are these romantic recipes, you ask? For those of you who don't have access to the World Wide Web and are forced to use this book as a pale substitute, we'll share our favorite one with you. Forget filet mignon. Forget chocolate truffles. Forget oysters on the half shell. Think mashed potatoes. Now don't get all skeptical; we're not talking about plain old mashed potatoes—we're talking about mashed potatoes *with carrots and onions!* We don't know about you, but nothing gets us in an amorous mood like a nice, big dollop of mashed potatoes with carrots and onions. But, as they say, "Romance for one is not much fun." (In point of fact, nobody says that—but it sounded catchy.) So we decided to try out the recipe on our husband. [Authors' note: We'd like to make it clear that we don't really share a husband. That would be absurd; we live on opposite coasts. And one of us is a guy. We're using the editorial "we" here.]

At dinner we presented him with a heaping plate of MPWCAO! He ate his portion, went back for seconds, and said, "This isn't too bad." So far, so good. He finished his second helping. We waited for the romance to kick in. A heavy sigh escaped his lips, and he softly uttered the following words: "I'm having trouble with the code for my graphics-positioning routine." (Actually, that *is* a fairly romantic statement for him). Then he went and sat at his computer terminal for six hours. So much for romance.

We can't help thinking the recipe would have conjured up some romantic moments for Fabio. But heck, he could probably get romantic results if he served his date a plate of live mealworms (with or without ICBINB!). Maybe we'll try another recipe on the hubby next week. Perhaps some nice SPAMsicles.

Breakfast Cereals Online . . . They're G-R-R-EAT!

Why—we can almost hear you asking—are there nearly as many breakfast-cereal Web pages as SPAM pages? Because—you can almost hear us answering—they're a profoundly important wellspring of American culture. Surely these amazing statistics will silence any doubts you may have as to this food's significance:

✧ The cereal industry uses 816 million pounds of sugar per year, enough to coat you and all other Americans with over three pounds of sugar.

- If laid end to end, the 2.7 billion empty cereal boxes from one year's U.S. consumption would stretch to the moon and back. (At first we were going to suggest that this might be a way for NASA to save money; astronauts could just climb up to the moon on all those cereal boxes. But, at $4.75 a box, this plan is undoubtedly more expensive than the current space program. Back to the drawing board.)
- The average American eats about 160 bowls of cereal every year, making the U.S. fourth in per capita cereal consumption. (Ireland, England, and Australia out-eat us in cereal, but it's not over till the fat lady sings.)
- 66 percent of Americans start each morning with a bowl of cereal. 30 percent eat toast, 28 percent eat eggs, 28 percent have coffee. Fewer than 10 percent have pancakes, sausage, bagels, or French toast. (We note that the totals equal far more than 100 percent, speaking of fat ladies singing.)

Once you take a moment to let these startling facts sink in, we're confident that you'll agree with the creators of the **Breakfast Cereal Hall of Fame** (http://www.cereal.com/index.html), who conclude that "koo-koo for Cocoa Puffs" and "silly rabbit" are better known than the National Anthem, that characters such as Tony the Tiger and Cap'n Crunch are more recognizable than any American political leader and are at least as trustworthy, and that, if you really think about it, "cereal was responsible for the rise of human civilization."

A few merry hours spent in the labyrinth of this reverent site will surely convince you that breakfast cereal is much more than just a food. It's a barometer of American pop culture: "From All-Bran to Cap'n Crunch, from Babe Ruth to Michael Jordan, from Jack Armstrong to Super Mario Brothers, the cereal aisle is a true and accurate reflection of America's cultural psyche." If that's true, we shudder to think what the popularity of Ninja Turtles or Fruity Pebbles says about America's cultural psyche.

Cereal is also a barometer of fashion. In fact, these style-conscious Web pages even offer instructions for creating your own Froot-Loops Chuck Taylor All Star Hi Top Sneakers. It's not for us to reveal the secret of creating these dramatic fashion statements—we'll let you visit the Web for that—but we will say that it involves a pair of sneakers, a tube of Aleene's Tacky Glue, and a box of Froot Loops. (A tip: "Do not use Elmer's glue. It is too moist and tends to shrink the Froot Loops into unrecognizable cereal shrivels.")

Froot Loops fashion statement

The Hall of Fame is filled with intriguing tidbits that bring the otherwise dry subject of cereal to life. Take the tale of Marky Maypo, the little four-year-old mascot who says (or said, in the 1950s), "I want my Maypo!" Little Marky was the creation of John Hubley, a former Disney animator who had worked on such non-cereal projects as Pinocchio, Fantasia, Bambi, and Dumbo. A company called Heublein hired Hubley—we're guessing because their names were so similar—to salvage the sinking sales of Maypo, a maple-syrup flavored hot cereal.

The ad Hubley came up with featured Marky, a rough 'n' ready little cartoon cowboy, sitting at the breakfast table while his dad cajoles him into eating his hot mush. The campaign increased sales of Maypo 78 percent and prompted millions of American kids to yell, "I want my Maypo!" Alas, Heublein and Hubley began to clash shortly thereafter, fighting over such issues as merchandising schemes for their new Marky character. They parted ways in 1960, but little Marky's legacy lives on in such modern slogans as "I want my MTV!"

More fascinating still is the sobering story of Sylvester Graham, hailed by Ralph Waldo Emerson as the "prophet of bran bread and pumpkins." Graham was, in fact, America's first health nut. There he was, in 1824, 160 years before modern America's recent bran craze, lecturing everywhere he went, "Put back the bran!" Not only did Graham become a national celebrity, but in 1992, General Mills named a wholesome new cereal after him—called S. W. Graham. (Unfortunately, General Mills's "I want my S. W. Graham!" ad campaign was a dismal failure, and that particular cereal rapidly faded into obscurity.)

Perhaps it's just as well that Graham's other major health beliefs aren't quite as well remembered today: mustard causes insanity; eating meat leads to masturbation; feather beds eventually kill you; and "disproportionate exercise of the brain leads to a general debility of the genital organs." (In other words, smart people have fewer children. Could that explain America's declining SAT scores?)

But the Breakfast Cereal Hall of Fame doesn't have a monopoly on cereal-related information on the Web. There's also **Flake World** (http://www. flake.com). Much as it might sound like ground zero for every creepy, unstable ex-girlfriend or ex-boyfriend you've ever had, it is, in fact, "your cyber-cereal picture gallery and shopping mall."

Truth to tell, "shopping mall" is the operative term here: the proprietor, Scott Bruce, intends to get rich selling you old cereal boxes over the Internet. Now, we've all got a few old cereal boxes in our cupboards—but Mr. Bruce's are *really* old. Decades old. 1960s old. Some typical products from this catalog of Items You'll Never See In L.L. Bean: "*1960 Post Sugar Crisp with bear bowl and mug offer*—Full & clean box, $99. Full & dented box, $75. Empty & mouse-holed box, $45; Empty, mouse-holed, and dented box, $29. Prices do not include shipping and handling." Or mice.

Sure, you laugh. $100 for an old piece of cardboard? Has this guy eaten one too many bowls of Cocoa Puffs, or what?

The only reason we're not laughing right along with you is that he's done it before. Scott Bruce is the very same guy who, in the late '80s, created the Vintage Lunch Box craze, appearing on *ABC World News* and the *Today* show, becoming the personal Vintage Lunch Box guru to Peter Max, Bruce Willis, and Mark Hamill, and selling his collection of old lunch boxes for hundreds or thousands of dollars apiece. (See **Land of the Lunch Boxes** at http://www2.ari.net/home/kholcomb/lunch.html for a look at lunchboxes throughout the ages.)

It's almost enough to make us want to buy a few old Quisp boxes to start our own collections. Who knows? Someday we, too, may get to meet Mark Hamill.

But listen: these Web sites embrace the history, psychology, and commerce of cereal. Perhaps we're placing too much significance on the fragile, essential-vitamin-enhanced shoulders of the mere mortal breakfast cereal. Perhaps we shouldn't over-intellectualize; perhaps it's enough just to read the box, as millions of Americans with nothing else to read during breakfast have discovered.

And indeed, thanks to the miracle of high-speed data transmission, you can now, during breakfast, read the boxes of cereal brands *other* than the one you're actually eating (be careful not to dribble any Maypo into your keyboard). That appears to be the founding principle behind **Crunchy Stuff** (http://www.ice.net/~crunch).

Upon arriving at this page, you may be confounded by the complete lack of text. What is this? All graphics? Just a bunch of thumbnail-sized cereal box pictures? Yes, exactly—60 of them, neatly arrayed, awaiting your artistic and discerning eye.

As the lone instruction sagely points out, "click on box to see it larger." Here's one example.

OK's: The Poor Man's Alpha-Bits

Our one regret is that you're allowed to read only the front of these boxes (although the "special offer inside!" is described for you in each case). The world waits for virtual-reality software to become commonplace before you'll be able to turn these boxes around, read the ingredients, cut out and collect the UPC bar code panels, and scrabble around inside the sugary pellets trying to find the cellophane-wrapped free prize while listening to an audio file of your mom saying, "Get your hand out of there! That's disgusting!"

Would You Like Fries with That?

Let's say you're traveling in Japan and get a hankering for some french fries. No problem. You whip out your Personal Digital Assistant, log on to the Internet, and go to **The Official French Fries Page** (http://www.selectware. com/fries/). There you'll learn that "french fry" is pronounced "foo-rai-doh poh-tay-toh" (who says Japanese is a difficult language?) and that in Japan, fries are served with ketchup, mayo, and perhaps a slice of lemon. Of course, french fries are not part of the traditional Japanese diet. Japanese diners much prefer strips of raw potato, or "poh-tay-toh su-shi." (Well, OK, we made up that last part.) You learn other useful facts about fries here as well, including the roles of Thomas Jefferson and Charles Dickens in the history of french fries.

If you hunger for more information about french fries—as well as other fast foods—a visit to **Fast Food Facts** (http://www.olen.com/food) should satisfy you. Simply choose your favorite fast-food restaurant from the handy pop-up menu (Arby's, Pizza Hut, Wendy's — what have you) or search for key words ("fried" would be a pretty good bet), and this miraculous calculator instantly displays just exactly how close each menu item will bring you to complete arterial blockage.

How else, for example, would you know that Chicken McNuggets consist of *57 percent pure fat?* Or that you can eat two scoops of Baskin Robbins' Pralines 'n' Cream ice cream and get the same amount of fat you'd get from eating a single Big Mac? Or that the Subway visitor who, trying to be health-conscious, orders a tuna salad will ingest an incredible 68 grams of fat—about the equivalent of *four* bags of White Castle onion rings, 10 Extra Tasty Crispy Chicken Drumsticks from KFC, six Taco Bell tacos, or 10 Wendy's grilled chicken sandwiches?

This handy little grossout calculator's figures come, we're told, from that best-known of nutritional authorities, the Minnesota Attorney General's Office. And what does the MAGO declare to be the single most caloric food morsel available in fast-food America today? Burger King's Double Whopper with Cheese, weighing in at an unbelievable 950 calories. Would you like a defibrillator with that?

Where Food Goes When It Dies

"Hey Heather! It's your turn to fight the rump roast!" So begins Kevin Greggain's **Rude Things in My Fridge** page (http://www.wbm.ca/users/kgreggai /html/fridge.html). Kevin is a veritable Prince of Putrefaction, a Duke of Decay. And he has decided to share the disgusting contents of his refrigerator with us. Thanks, Kevin.

We wonder who Heather is, since elsewhere on his page he states—and we have no reason to doubt him—that "No woman in her right mind will put up with my habits." We must assume, then, that Heather is either not a woman (perhaps she's a pet), or she's—what's the politically correct term?—one taco short of a combination plate.

Kevin gives us monthly photographic glimpses of former foodstuffs found in his refrigerator, beginning in May 1995. The photos have titles such as "Mushrooms?," "Apple?," "Cheese?," "Bowl?," and so on. If you dare to peruse the photos, you'll understand why the titles have question marks.

Kevin isn't a complete slob, though; his Web page is very nicely designed, with a festive border of rats and rotting food, some animated flies, and a soundtrack that includes a food-curdling shriek. With all the work he put into that page, he probably didn't have time to clean the fridge. Or throw away the gutted fish that sat on his balcony for five months. Or wash last year's dishes. (While his site proudly displays several awards, we noticed that the Good Housekeeping Seal of Approval is not among them.)

But wait! There's hope for the rotting food in Kevin's refrigerator. At **The BrainMatters Great Tomato Experiment** at http://www.discovery.ca/ @discovery/bmatter.htm, you can read about an experiment on the effects of prayer on sick tomatoes. The Canadian Discovery Channel ran a "scientifically controlled" experiment in which some tomatoes were injected with a blight. Volunteers then surrounded the infected tomatoes and encouraged them to get better. Members of the TV audience were also invited to send their healing prayers tomatoward.

Something's rotten in Kenmore.

The results? The wounds on some of the tomatoes that received prayers were smaller than the wounds on a control group of tomatoes that were left to fend for themselves.

Therefore, dear reader, we urge you to direct your kind thoughts and prayers toward the unfortunate vegetables in Kevin's refrigerator. And toward poor Heather, whoever she may be.

Greetings from
The Weird Wide Web

Pop! Goes the Culture

Like television, the Web was seen in its early days as a wondrous new world. A little glowing box in every home would dispense a wealth of educational, scientific, and cultural content. It would be a universally available resource, accessible to the masses at an affordable price. But, as with television, much of the Web's content devolved into, shall we say, less than intellectually stimulating topics; the nadir was reached when people published sites showing the contents of their wallets (http://condor.stcloud.msus.edu/~nordem01/wallet.html).

Sure, the Web still has its equivalent of PBS, where you can visit **the Louvre** (http://mistral.culture.fr/louvre/) or read **Shakespeare's sonnets** (http://www.ludweb.com/msff/sonnets/sonnets.html)—but it also has its share of plebeian sites analogous to "Mr. Ed " or **"The Honeymooners"** (http://www.honeymooners.net/). Like it or not, *The Brady Bunch* is as much a part of our culture as *Romeo and Juliet*. Probably more so.

You can use the Web to take a virtual vacation, learn a foreign language, or view works of art. So what if the vacation is to an abandoned missile silo or an endless series of all-night restaurants, the foreign language is Klingon, and the artwork is photos of Barbie dolls? We're at the end of the Twentieth Century; we've lowered our standards. Let's face it, these days you're much more likely to impress someone by knowing where to find the world's largest thermometer than by quoting *Hamlet* (unless you can quote it in Klingon, that is).

In this chapter we cover the major aspects of our culture, such as it is, including Art, Music (sort of), Literature, the Cinema, Religion, Language, and *The Brady Bunch*. We come not to bury Mike Brady but to praise him.

The Cinema: Alternative Views

Scott Williams and Alistair B. Fraser host a site called **The Bagpipes Go to the Movies** (http://www.ems.psu.edu/~fraser/PipesMovies.html). These guys don't take their bagpipes into movie theaters, mind you; it's bad enough when people talk while you're trying to watch a movie. Rather, the site lists dozens of movies in which bagpipes are featured. The films include obviously bagpipeworthy fare such as *Braveheart* and *Brigadoon*, as well as movies one would not necessarily associate with bagpipes, such as *Ferris Bueller's Day Off* and *Ghostbusters II*. Needless to say, this site provides an invaluable service: you can consult the list to make sure you don't inadvertently go to a movie that has bagpipe music in it.

For another unique perspective on the movies, you might want to visit **Dermatology In the Cinema** (http://www.skinema.com). Then again, you might not. Dermatologist/film buff Vail Reese can't help but notice actors' skin conditions when he goes to the movies (he must have had a swell time watching *Elephant Man*), and he's decided to share his observations with you. While the aforementioned Messrs. Williams and Frasier are entranced by the strains of bagpipe music in *Ghostbusters II*, Vail Reese is busy looking at Bill Murray's acne scars.

This site is actually quite educational. Here you'll learn, via before-and-after photos of Robert Redford and Brigitte Bardot, that prolonged sun exposure can wreak havoc on the skin (but that you'll still look pretty good, in a leathery sort of way, if you started out looking like Bardot or Redford). You'll see photographic evidence that Richard Gere has a birthmark called a Becker's nevus, and that Arnold Schwarzenegger had a mole removed from his jaw. You'll learn that W. C. Fields's bulbous nose is an example of rhinophyma, which can occur after years of untreated adult acne. You'll also learn that Michael Jackson claims he has vitiligo, a disease that attacks skin-pigmentation cells, resulting in skin lightening. (Uh-huh. And he no doubt also suffers from antirhinophyma, which makes the nose grow progressively smaller.)

Dr. Reese points out that skin disfigurements (burns, scars, or diseases) are often used to make movie bad guys look scary or evil, and that this can reinforce prejudices people already have concerning skin diseases. So, the next time you see a hideously scarred villain in a movie, have a little sympathy and compassion—unless he's playing the bagpipes.

What's on TV?

As even the novice Web surfer knows, the Web occasionally provides *practical* information—but its true calling is the advancement of American pop culture icons. It should come as no surprise, then, that America's most beloved implausible family, the Brady Bunch, should be represented disproportionately on the Web. For example, there's **The Unofficial Brady Bunch Home Page** (exhaustive, and exhausting, trivia, right down to blueprints of the Brady house—http://www.teleport.com/~btucker/bradys.shtml); **Jeff's Brady Bunch Gallery** (pix! pix! pix! at http://weber.u.washington.edu/~schell/brady. html); **The Brady Bunch Trivia Challenge** ("What was Bobby's frog's name? What's the name of the dentist Marcia had a crush on? What color did Greg's hair turn with Bobby's hair tonic? When Zaccariah Brown locks the Bradys in the town jail, who did he say was once locked in there?"—http://www.mtwinc.com/~brettsch/Trivia/Brady_Bunch); **Growing Up Brady** (cast member Barry Williams, author of the best-seller *Growing Up Brady: I Was A Teenage Greg*, gives "an insider's perspective on the whirlwind life of a teen idol and beyond" at http://t-e-i.com/growingupbrady.html); and many more.

Perhaps the most encyclopedic trove of Bradynalia is, naturally, the **Encyclopedia Brady** (http://www.primenet.com/~dbrady). Written by one David Brady (no relation), it's a compendium of every person, place, or thing ever mentioned in the 117 *Brady Bunch* episodes—from Albuquerque ("city where

Mike's aunt lives") to *You Too Can Be a Chef* ("book Mike reads in order to help Marcia earn her cooking badge"). Where else could you learn what car the Brady Bunch drove (Chrysler station wagon, license plate Y 18 078)? How else could you recall the mordant, all-too-real dialog ("Cindy's real neat—for a girl, I mean")? And where else could a single encyclopedia entry ("PRIVATE! KEEP OUT") help you relive an entire *Brady Bunch* plotline ("Sign on the boys' clubhouse. Jan steals it and hangs it on the girls' bedroom door")?

And now for a commercial break . . .

Human beings are capable of one certain facial expression, a cross between helpless confusion and contempt, rarely seen except following a Mentos commercial on TV. Surely you've seen those ads—hopelessly kitschy, contrived mini-dramas in which a sassy, good-looking, Germanic teenager flaunts the disrespect of the older generation as the Abba-esque jingle plays: "Fresh goes better, Mentos freshness, fresh goes better with Mentos, fresh and full of life! Mentos, the freshmaker!"

If, for some unfathomable reason, you're intrigued by these ads (or the chewy roll candies they promote), tune your dial to http://www.mentos.com, the **Mentos** page. The highlights of this exploration of the Mentos mystique are the complete synopses of the ten goofy ads, written in a strangely enthusiastic style that seems to fit perfectly the Mentos ethos:

> While crossing the street, a teen is separated from his friends, and nearly from his legs, by an over-anxious motorist. Finding himself needing to traverse the street, he thanks his lucky stars he remembers the freshmaker. His supply is reduced by one, but his freshness is increased exponentially. Opening the rear door, he climbs through the auto, while the driver looks over his shoulder in astonishment. Upon exiting, the youth shrugs at the motorist, Mentos in hand. Although a bit shaken, the passenger acknowledges the carefree youths with an approving glance that seems to say, "Wait till the wife hears of my brush with freshness!"

True to the Europeanishness of the ads, it turns out that Mentos come from Holland, but that the same commercials are shown worldwide. That, we think, explains why they have no dialogue, and suggests that these commercials must be baffling people all over the world. (We wonder how they play in, say New York City or Miami, where your average motorist would probably not be amused to have a long-haired youth burst into his or her car. Anyone in the U.S. who chortled approvingly at a candy-wielding thug would be declared *non compos mentos*.)

Dig deeper into the Mentos site, and you find a list of TV shows that have parodied the ads (*Letterman, Saturday Night Live,* Janeane Garofolo); a list of Mentos vocabulary (*Cementos*—what Mentos become after 3 weeks in your glove compartment); new acronyms based on Mentology (*FAFOL*—Fresh And Full Of Life); complete ingredients lists, by flavor (*Mixed Fruit:* sugar, glucose syrup, hydrogenated coconut oil, gelatin, dextrin, natural and artificial flavor, gum arabic, coloring); and, of course, the Mentos Gallery, a well-stocked museum of famous paintings that have been doctored to include a roll of our favorite international candy.

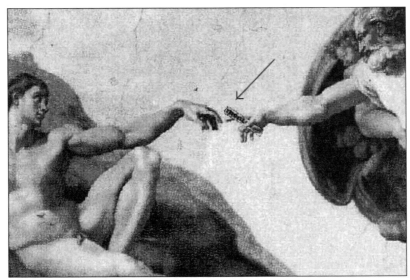

A little-known corner of Michelangelo's famous Sistine chapel ceiling

Spend a few moments chewing on this infectiously sassy site, and you, too, will be FAFOL. Or perhaps FATWOE (Fuming At The Waste Of Electrons).

Learn a Foreign Language, Eggplanthead

The Web has virtually limitless potential as a tool for teaching languages. None of the sites listed here comes close to realizing that potential, we're sorry to say, but you can learn some handy phrases in the language of your choice (as long as you choose Italian or Swedish . . . or Klingon).

At the **Learn to Speak Italian** site (http://www.eat.com/learn-italian/index. html), Professore Antonio not only provides useful phrases in a number of categories (travel, romance, food, the family, and so on), but he speaks the phrases aloud for you, thanks to the wonders of digital audio. Here you can learn how to say things such as "I would like two tickets for tonight's opera, please" *(Vorrei due biglietti per l'opera di questa sera, per favore)*, "Has anyone ever told you that you have a head like an eggplant?" *(C'è qualcuno che Le ha mai detto che ha una testa come una melanzana?)*, and "You snore like a buzzsaw, but I adore you anyway" *(Russi come una sega meccanica, ma ti adoro nondimeno)*. That's amore!

Once you've mastered Italian, you can move on to Swedish. Well, Swedish cursing, anyway. "In eight lessons you can learn how to cuss in Swedish like a sailor." How can you pass that up? At **Cursing In Swedish** (http://www.santesson.com/enginvek.html) you learn how to spew vile invective such as "Damn, I missed the bus!" *(Jävlar, jag missade bussen!)* and "Blast it, I will not pay the parking fine!" *(Så sjutton att jag tänker betala p-böterna!)*. (Swedish sailors apparently don't cope too well on dry land.) If you click on a phrase you hear it spoken, at which point it becomes painfully obvious that Swedish is not a world-class cussing language. Its melodious tones and lilting cadences just don't lend themselves to swearing. Even a phrase such as "I dropped the *%@*# soap!" lacks conviction in Swedish: the curser in the sound file doesn't sound even slightly miffed. Must be all those soothing massages.

Now, if you want a great language for swearing, try Klingon, which you can learn to speak and write at **The Klingon Language Institute** (http://www. kli.org/KLIhome.html).

Klingon is a harsh and guttural language and is, unlike that wimpy Swedish, an excellent choice for cursing. ("When speaking Klingon, be sure to speak *forcefully.* Some of the sounds may make the person you're talking to a little wet.") Just listening to a benign phrase such as "What's happening?" *(qaStaH nuq?)* sends chills down your spine. And an insult such as "Your mother had a smooth forehead!" *(Hab SoSlI' Quch!)* is enough to send you packing back to your own galaxy.

Unlike most languages, the origins of Klingon are easy to trace: the Klingon language was created by Marc Okrand for the *Star Trek* movies. So what if Klingons are fictitious aliens? The Klingon Language Institute is a serious enterprise. Founded in 1992, the Institute now has more than 1,000 members. It is incorporated as a domestic nonprofit corporation within the Commonwealth of Pennsylvania and federally recognized as a nonprofit organization under section 501(c)3 of the IRS code. (We can only hope they fill out their tax returns in Klingon glyphs.) The Institute offers a quarterly journal, a dictionary, a phrasebook, a correspondence course, and a Klingon typeface. Scholars are even now translating the Bible into Klingon, and a translation of *Hamlet* was recently published. Are these folks nuts? *peDoghQo'!* (Don't be silly!)

If you don't have a knack for languages, you can at least expand the boundaries of your native tongue by learning some Mafia slang. The **Mobspeak Glossary** (http://www.gotti.com/glossary.html) is an offshoot (as it were) of The John Gotti Tribute Page, which is the creation of Ravenna Angelini (not her real name, we suspect). Ravenna's turn-ons: alpha males, pinkie rings, Lincoln Town Cars, computer upgrades. Her mission: to pay homage to "all-around nice guy" John Gotti (currently serving a life sentence at the Marion Control Unit Federal Penitentiary).

What good will Mafia slang do you? Well, let's say, for example, that "your shylock (who brags about being a big earner for the borgata) is threatening to do a piece of work because you haven't paid your vig, and you don't know what the hell he's talking about?" Don't sweat it, babbo; you may be an empty suit, but maybe if you learn to talk the talk you can convince the capo you're a stand-up guy. Capische?

Art for Barbie's Sake

You tell *us* which is most disturbing: that, in 1981, Dean Brown's daughter gave him a Barbie doll for his birthday — or that Brown became obsessed with Barbies, photographing them in a fantasy world of everyday life? Or is it most disturbing that, 15 years and 300 photos later, his Barbie photos have been exhibited as *art* in galleries from Washington to California?

Regardless of whether Brown, his daughter, or the art community strikes you as the most deviant, Brown's weird little hobby is on display at **The Barbie Chronicles** (http://www.erols.com/browndk). In page after page of color photos, Barbie, Ken, and her pert and perfect plastic Barbie friends are depicted in heartwarming slices of everyday life: going to the prom, getting married, getting abducted by King Kong, and so on.

The highlight is the Barbie's History of Art pages. Here, Mr. Brown has painstakingly posed and costumed Barbie to resemble famous paintings through the ages. They're all here: Degas (Barbie at the Barre). Whistler (Portrait of Barbie's Mother). Rubens (The Judgment of Barbie). Toulouse-Lautrec (Moulin Rouge — Barbie Edition).

When you pose Barbies in an effort to emulate Manet or Degas, at least you're trying to duplicate greatness. It's quite another story at **The Museum of Bad Art** (http://glyphs.com/moba), which is an actual collection of actual bad paintings based in a Boston gallery. But MOBA is so much more than a gallery; this beloved institution has become been repeatedly reinvented as a CD-ROM, a newsletter, occasional exhibitions, and even a book, so that ever more bad art fans can cherish this deliciously pathetic collection.

As Scott Wilson, the curator, notes, "The pieces in the MOBA collection range from the work of talented artists that have gone awry, to works of exuberant artists barely in control of the brush. What they all have in common is a special quality that sets them apart from the merely incompetent."

As celebrators of the worst of the Web, we, of course, toast MOBA's efforts. And we encourage you to stroll its virtual gallery online, drinking in works such as *Lucy in the Field With Flowers* ("What is Norman Mailer's head doing on grandma's body, and are those crows or F-16's skimming the hills?") and *Eileen* (stolen during an exhibition; "Mr. Wilson, the museum's curator, has offered a $6.50 reward for any information leading to the safe return of *Eileen* to the MOBA walls").

Lucy in the Field With Flowers
© Museum of Bad Art

Eileen
© Museum of Bad Art

Literature from A to B

If you've ever indulged in the guilty pleasure of reading a romance novel, do we have the site for you! **Romance Writer** (http://www.islandnet.com/~zam/aha/romance.htm) generates steamy prose at the click of a button, creating as many bodice-rippers as you can stomach (er, enjoy).

Here's a sample:

Encounter Under the Influence
*Waiting alone in the midst of her uncle's
grotesque curios, with the rhythmic
strumming of Pedro's guitar wafting in
from outside, Alicia — she who had always
seemed so cold! — thought once more of
Edwin, the man who had taught her how
to feel. He was now, according to the
message on the dagger, away again on
safari.*

*Then came an inrush of cool air as the
door was flung open, and she leapt to her
feet with hope — and alarm — in her eyes.
He was here! "We marry tonight, my
angel — my porcelain angel!" he said
quietly, signalling his porters to withdraw,
and as the horror of these last months
vanished in a blaze of joy, she vowed
never again to do anything spiteful, foolish
or immature.*

Oh! Our limpid eyes are brimming with jewel-like tears at the beauty of that stirring denouement!

For another perspective on Literature, see **Bad Teen Angst Poetry** (is there any other kind of teen poetry?) at http://www.cyberperk.com/angst/angst. htm. The creators of this site realize that everyone, at one point or another, during a bout of teenage hormone-induced wretchedness, has written some really awful poems. Remember? Two in the morning, pounding away on your dad's old typewriter, shunned by the opposite sex, misunderstood by your parents, your face a welter of pimples, burning to distill into poetry the raw despair, the alienation, and the ridicule that a person of your superior intellect and heightened emotional state was forced to endure from lesser beings. Ah, those were the days! You might have even stashed a notebook full of these gems in a box of high school mementos in your parents' basement — a notebook that your parents are reading even now, tears of hysterical laughter streaming down their wizened cheeks.

The keepers of this site invite you to air your bad teen angst poetry, which they claim will dissipate the shame you feel for writing the stuff in the first place. (You'll want to submit them anonymously, of course, unless you enjoy being publicly humiliated.) If nothing else, reading the poems here—representative titles: "Drugged Reflections," "Abyss," "Nothingness," "Alone," "Stranded," "Tears," "Black Hole," "Love Sells You Cold," "You Don't Understand," "Before the Prom," "Grapefruit Tears," "Lawnmower of Life"—will make you realize that other teens wrote poems just as god-awful as yours. Maybe even worse. It's a good feeling.

From "Boys"
the heart is not a plaything
the heart is not a toy
but if you want it broken
just give it to a boy . . .
— Anon., age 16

From "Why"
. . . I know sometime the rain must fall
And birds must leave their nests,
The stream cannot forever run
Nor the sun stay always abreast.
But why must fences be put up
When you thought you were free!
Why must the song hit a wrong note¿¿¡!
Why here, why now . . . Why ME¿¿!!!!
— Anon., age 16

And the one that pretty much sums it all up:

"Philosophy"
Life is a never ending abyss
of hatred and despair
Full of let down upon horrible let down
and a few brief moments of insane hope
which are instantly crushed by reality
from the day we are born
until the day we finally die.
— Anon., age 15

We're not positive, but we're pretty sure the tortured teen who wrote "Philosophy" grew up to write a poem called "Spleen," which is quoted in the next section.

A Musical Interlude

How can we begin to describe the indescribable tragicomic horror of the **Captain James T. Kirk Sing-Along Page** (http://www.loskene.com/singalong/kirk.html)? Perhaps we should begin by noting the fallacy of the title itself: it's William Shatner (the actor), not James T. Kirk (the character), doing the singing. Come to think of it, he's not actually singing, either. Since Mr. Shatner is, whatever his other abilities, entirely talent-free when it comes to carrying a tune, he pretty much just speaks, as a professional choir does the actual singing behind him. A more accurate, albeit less attractive, name would have been "The Mr. William J. Shatner Speak-Along in Disbelief Page."

In a spectacular career-judgment error, Mr. Shatner recorded an album in 1968, at the peak of his *Star Trek* popularity, when his agents were no doubt confident that anything Bill did would sell. The result was "The Transformed Man," a tragic testament to one actor's ego. The Captain James T. Kirk Sing-Along Page presents the story of this album, the complete list of lyrics, and several hideous sound files.

We would be hard-pressed to choose a favorite from among the seven excerpts, which include "Mr. Tambourine Man," "Lucy in the Sky With Diamonds," and "Theme from Cyrano." Imagine, if you will, Mr. Shatner emoting his way through "Mr. Tambourine Man." The stunning finale goes like this:

Kirk: . . . in the jingle . . . [sounds like he's choking on a tribble] . . . jangle . . . mornin' I'll come . . . followin' you!

Chorus: Hey, Mr. Tambourine Man? Hey, Mr. Tambourine Man?

Kirk: Mr. Tambourine Man . . . Mr. Tambourine Man? Hey ! . . . Mr. Tambourine Man? Mr. Tambourine Man? MR. TAMBOURINE MAAANNNN!!!!!!!

(To properly appreciate our use of seven exclamation points, you have to hear it. Shatner literally screams the final words as the orchestra and chorus abruptly disappear. It's the anguished shriek of one lonely soul alone in a vast, dark world.)

Then there's Mr. Shatner's suite of dramatic monologues. Set to '60s hokey pop/rock accompaniment, you get such hits as the soliloquy from *Hamlet* (the English version, not the Klingon translation mentioned earlier), a clip from *King Henry V*, and a veritable cornucopia of painfully bad poetry. Listen, for example, to the torment in Kirk's voice as he recites "Spleen" (imagine wild bells ringing in the background):

Then suddenly the bells jerk wildly and hurled to the sky a horrible SHRIEK, like some wandering and landless spirit, wailing in despair!

And long hearses, without drums, without music, file slowly through my soul. Hope, vanquished, weeps and despotic agony plants on my bent skull, its flag of BLACK!

But our favorite, the one that's certain to haunt us long into our fading years (or drive us into therapy), is Mr. Shatner's interpretation of "Lucy in the Sky with Diamonds." Here, he speaks in tortured bursts (to get the idea, think Kirk saying, "Must . . . reach . . . transporter room . . ."), slurring some words, yelping others, and generally doing his best impersonation of a late-'60s druggie.

Lest you find our critique of Mr. Shatner's sole foray into pop music a tad harsh, let us hasten to add that his fellow cast members did no better. Turns out many *Star Trek* alumni have made similarly unsuccessful attempts to cross over from the surprisingly unrelated fields of sci-fi TV acting to '60s rock stardom. On the Sing-Along Page you can also listen to Scotty crooning a Scottish lullaby, Uhura singing a lick from her debut album (turns out she actually has a voice), and Data (from *Star Trek: The Next Generation*) singing "Toot-Toot-Tootsie, Goodbye."

None of these can touch, however, the pure agonizing awfulness of the singing efforts of Leonard Nimoy, best known to Trekkies as Mr. Spock. The Sing-Along Page offers a clip of a song called "Illogical," a shrewd attempt to capitalize on his *Star Trek* character's fame. Listening to this gross mismatch of our favorite repressed Vulcan and funky, '60s rock accompaniment provides the same greasy thrill as hearing Bob Dole sing "Do Ya Think I'm Sexy."

From far beyond the galaxies, I've traveled to this place
To study the behavior patterns of the human race.
And I find them . . . Highly illogical!

Take the case of your automobiles.
Greatest invention since man invented wheels.
Hydromatic overdrive, four on the floor,
Pushbutton windows, pushbutton doors,
Double-barreled carburetors rush you any place
But you never can find a parking space!
Highly illogical!

Totally . . . completely . . . absolutely . . . irrevocably . . . highly . . .
Illogical!

Leave it to Mr. Spock to make such trenchant, witty observations about the foibles and frailties of our human condition.

Beam us up!

Another aspiring crooner is Elizabeth Tashjian, also known as "The Nut Lady." We're talking walnuts and pistachios here, mind you—The Nut Lady is the longtime proprietress of the Nut Museum in Old Lyme, Connecticut. At **The Nut Lady's Home Page** (http://www.roadsideamerica. com/nut/index.html) you'll find information about the Nut Museum (and the cruel bureaucrats who tried to close it down, claiming it was "infested with squirrels"), which celebrates that unsung hero of nutrition, the nut. The museum includes many of the Nut Lady's paintings, poems, and sculptures, allowing visitors to come away with not only a heightened appreciation of nuts but a more tolerant outlook on life as well: "The Nut Lady points to a painting of nutcrackers and nuts floating in what looks to be amniotic fluid. 'In the outside world, nutcrackers are the nuts' mortal enemy,' she explains. 'Here, nuts and nutcrackers can be friends.'"

The World's Largest Nut
© 1997 roadsideamerica.com, Kirby, Smith, Wilkins

If you can't make it to the Nut Museum, you can at least visit the Web site and hear the Nut Lady sing two odes to nuts: "March of the Nuts" and "Nuts are Beautiful." Here's an excerpt from "Nuts are Beautiful":

O nobody ever thinks about nuts
Nuts can be so beautiful if looked aright
Take them home and handle them properly, artistically
And feel a new taste being born

O nuts have a curious history and lore
Nuts grew in the one Garden of Eden
They've been nourishing man since creation began
Nuts are fresh tokens of primeval life!

Ah! A welcome counterpoint to Kirk's and Spock's angst-riddled diatribes.

Exploding Celebrities

In our electronic age, we don't choose our superheroes on the basis of strength or intellect; instead, we choose them on the basis of media saturation. Our role models are no longer the Supermans and Moseses: they're the Bill Gateses and Rush Limbaughs. These supergurus dominate the newscasts, the radio shows, the lunchroom conversation . . . and you, the lowly non-superstar, are condemned to live with these media darlings three inches from your face.

Or are you? At **The Exploding Head Page** (http://www.king.net/gilmore/head/), you're offered the chance to indulge your every childish revenge fantasy. To put it bluntly, you can explode people's heads. As the intro puts it: "No detailed explanation is really necessary, and none would truly suffice to describe the awe-inspiring glory of this page. But one theme runs through it all: the exploding heads of, well, of people whose heads you've always wanted to see explode."

You're offered a choice of several satisfying-to-detonate media figures: Boris Yeltsin, Bob Dole, Rush Limbaugh, and, by popular demand, Bill Gates. And then there's Tom Hanks. Why on earth would anyone want to watch lovable old Tom Hanks' head explode? Two words: Forrest Gump.

All you have to do is click the picture of the person you'd like to explode. You don't get sound, you don't get a movie—such multimedia smarts would be far too sophisticated for this most infantile pleasure. Instead, you're shown several still frames of the head in various stages of dismemberment. Here's Mr. Limbaugh exploding—you might call it the ultimate head rush:

Hot air builds up and...bang!

As you can imagine, not everyone finds this virtual massacre amusing. The U.S. Secret Service was particularly unenthused about the Bob Dole head-explosion option. In fact, they paid a visit to Daniel Wayne Burford (aka Gilmore), the creator of the Exploding Heads page, no doubt worried that he was a dangerous cult leader with a secret agenda to commit terrorist acts on presidential candidates and overweight talk-show hosts. (You can read a gripping account of this exchange on the site, complete with a scan of a real Secret Serviceman's business card!) After grilling poor Mr. Burford under hot fluorescent office lights for what seemed days (but was in fact about 20 minutes), they determined that he was harmless—tasteless, but harmless—and let him go.

The world was safe for juvenile splatter humor once again.

Religion Lite

If you're feeling guilty after exploding Tom Hanks' head, don't worry. The Web has plenty of religious sites where you can confess your sins and be absolved—without ever leaving your desk. Why not start out at the online **Confession Booth,** "Bringing the net to its knees since 1994" at http://anther.learning.cs.cmu.edu/priest.html. It's quick and easy: you simply pick a sin from a multiple-choice list (unfortunately for those of us with a depraved lifestyle, you can choose only one sin at a time). You can type in details if you wish, then press a button to transmit your confession, and a penance is issued. If you want to go public, you can submit your confession to the Scroll of Sin, where it will be available for all to see.

Unfortunately, when we submitted a confession we got a server error ("The server encountered an internal error or misconfiguration and was unable to complete your request"), which produced a severe crisis of faith.

To console ourselves, we paid a visit to **Prayers Heavenbound,** "The New Way to Pray" (http://www.primenet.com/~prayers/). This outfit uses the latest technology to "electronically beam prayers, hopes and dreams into space, into time, . . . into forever." (They claim that the radio waves that carry the messages "will endure until our present Universe ceases to exist," which is sure better than those puny lifetime guarantees some companies give you.)

Their equipment "accepts your letters or drawings, and launches them electronically at the speed of light on a powerful microwave radio beam into deep space. As soon as they are sent, they become available to be intercepted by God." (We sure hope their technology works better than that of the aforementioned Confession Booth.) Here's how it works:

- ✵ Your written prayer is fed into an optical scanner and converted by a computer into digital pulses.
- ✵ These digital pulses are transmitted into deep space as radio waves via a microwave transmitter. (Lest you doubt the signal will travel All the Way, rest assured that their system achieves an effective isotropic radiated power of 20 million watts.)

This amazing juxtaposition of science and religion costs only $9.95 per page. Sorry, no C.O.D.s.

Surf the Web and See the World

Whew! Bad art . . . teen angst . . . religion. This chapter's getting pretty heavy. Time to lighten up and plan a vacation. If you don't have the time or the money to take a real vacation, you can always take a virtual vacation via the World Wide Web. In keeping with the spirit of this book, we will eschew traditional destinations such as Rome or Paris and concentrate instead on some offbeat odysseys. Take, for example, the fellow who has made it his life's mission to visit as many Denny's restaurants as possible. Or maybe you'd prefer a janitor's-eye tour of Disney World, a look at some stoplights in Canada, or a visit to an old missile silo. Read on.

Jason Pfaff's fascination for the Denny's chain of 24-hour cheap eats can be only partly explained by his grandfather-chaperoned visits there as a wee lad and by his year working as a Denny's waiter. No, his problem is deeper: his stated goal in life is "to visit as many Denny's as possible before I die." At **Project: Denny's** (http://www.concentric.net/~p7a77/dennys), he chronicles his travels to Denny's restaurants throughout the land.

So many Denny's, so little time

Here, then, for the morbid and the bored, is a complete list of Denny's restaurant outlets visited by Mr. Pfaff in his quest. The dozens of branches are carefully organized by chronology, geographic region, and Denny's franchise number. Each visit is documented with photos, descriptions of waitresses, list of items ordered, and which of Mr. Pfaff's hapless friends were in attendance.

To heighten the challenge, Mr. Pfaff has two sub-goals during each Denny's visit. First, he tries to scam free stuff; usually, he says, "the wait-person is so relieved to have someone friendly to talk to for a change, s/he will just give me something." (Sample trophies: Denny's tie clip, Breakfast Values menu, Coke Pin, Lunch Basket Promotional Poster.) Second, at each Denny's visit, the author seeks to prove a pet theory: that every Denny's manager looks like the comedian Weird Al Yankovic (who, for the uninitiated, is "a tall scrawny guy with a dark mustache, silver rimmed glasses, and big curly black hair"). Mr. Pfaff says he's "a bit lenient on the specifics (i.e., the hair doesn't have to be curly, and the glasses can be a different color, and the employee doesn't have to be a manager), but there has to be a strong resemblance overall." Surprisingly, the majority of the Denny's documented on this Web site do indeed feature a Weird Al look-alike.

We can only wish good luck and godspeed to Mr. Pfaff and "Das Büs," the secondhand schoolbus he travels in. Who says today's youth lacks ambition?

Perhaps Mr. Pfaff will someday extend his Denny's journeys into Canada (yes, there are Denny's restaurants in Canada, according to contributors to his site). If so, he can contribute to Neil Enns's dream: to display photos of **Traffic Lights on the Trans-Canada Highway** (http://www. brandonu.ca/~ennsnr/Traffic/).

A stoplight in Manitoba

"Unfortunately," begins Mr. Enns's site, "I have neither the time nor the money to drive cross-country and take pictures of all the traffic lights. . . . That's why I'm asking for your help!" Mr. Enns is soliciting help from the worldwide community of Web users, who are asked to send any photos they might have of traffic lights on the highways that make up the Trans-Canada system. The response has not been overwhelming. So far, this site has half a dozen photos, all from the province of Manitoba—and all taken by Mr. Enns. But we're sure that travelers will rally and help Mr. Enns reach his lofty goal: to "eventually have pictures of all the traffic lights on the Trans-Canada Highway!"

For another monomaniacal look at the world, check out **The Trash Cans of Disney** (http://www.swt.edu/~CS22517/), the opus of a young man named Codie Smith. According to his bio, Codie Smith, like Leonardo da Vinci, is interested in a great many things. Unlike Leonardo da Vinci, however, Codie Smith is interested in the trash cans at Disney World. Mr. Smith, Renaissance Man, scholar, photographer, and part-time janitor, has taken it upon himself to present a custodian's-eye view of the Magic Kingdom.

"You do not generally pay a great deal of attention to the garbage cans around you. You should; you can learn a lot," begins Mr. Smith's treatise. You probably never noticed, for example, that the trash cans at Disney theme parks are painted to blend into their particular surroundings. Imagine, if you can, the incongruity of a rustic, pioneer-style trash can in Tomorrowland. Couldn't happen! Disney's "imagineers" wouldn't allow such a *faux pas*; the cans must adhere to each of the park's subthemes. In Tomorrowland's Starlight Cafe, for example, there's a futuristic talking trash can. "That's right folks. If you put your trash in the correct side of the can, it says neat little things like, 'Yum Yum.'" (We can only surmise that if you insert your trash incorrectly, the can says "Ha Ha!" and immediately vaporizes you.)

Here are some fascinating statistics, culled from Mr. Smith's research:

- There are 800 trash cans at the Magic Kingdom, 970 at EPCOT, and 450 at Disney/MGM Studios.

- There are about 120 different trash can designs.

- New cans (pre-painted) cost about $250 each. On many cans, however, Disney adds its own special, hand-painted touches, adding as much as $200 to the cost. "The most expensive cans are those disguised at tree stumps located on Tom Sawyer's Island (in the Magic Kingdom) and at the Fort Wilderness Campground. They ship at about $5,000 each!" And you thought those $2,000 Pentagon coffeemakers were expensive!

Fantasyland   Tomorrowland (pretty futuristic, eh?)

Disney World's all very nice (even its trashy side), but true adventurers prefer destinations that even professional imagineers could never imagine. Like abandoned missile silos, for example. The opening words of the **Abandoned Missile Silo Tour** (http://www.xvt.com/users/kevink/silo/) begin:

> PLEASE . . . DO NOT TRY TO ENTER ONE OF THESE SITES YOURSELF! WE WERE VIOLATING FEDERAL TRESPASSING LAWS BY VISITING THIS INSTALLATION. FELONY CHARGES WILL HAUNT YOU THE REST OF YOUR LIFE! HAD ONE OF US BEEN HURT BENEATH THE SURFACE, IT WOULD HAVE BEEN VERY DIFFICULT TO REMOVE THE VICTIM/BODY. THERE IS ALSO A SIGNIFICANT CHANCE THAT THE RADIOACTIVE GAS 'RADON' BUILDS UP DOWN THERE, TOO. WE HAVE BROUGHT THIS PHOTO-TOUR TO YOU SO THAT YOU WON'T HAVE TO GO THERE YOURSELF TO SEE IT.

Whew. Well, that's a blessing. Radon, schmadon—we're feeling a little woozy just from reading the disclaimer.

Danger! Danger! Don't look down — don't even breathe!

Anyway, if you're bold enough to proceed, by clicking and waiting for big photos to paint their way onto your screen, you can indeed take an impressive virtual tour of an abandoned missile silo. At each juncture, you can turn right, turn left, turn back, or (if you dare) push on deeper into the forbidden darkness. It's like playing *Myst,* except that the mystical abandoned world was constructed by the U.S. Government during the Cold War.

You eventually learn that what's left of Your Tax Dollars At Work is a bunch of flooded, pitch-black rooms filled with old rusty machinery. What keeps it interesting are the captions:

> Parts were dry and it was possible to kick up some dust. Asbestos is a dangerous carcinogen (it causes cancer). These underground sites have been known to have dioxin contamination, too. Also, most of the complex is lined with iron that has been rusting for decades. It would not be smart to enter this place without a breathing mask, clothes that you never intend to wear again, sturdy boots, a helmet with a light, sealed gloves, and a recent tetanus shot.

Suit yourself, but we're convinced; we put on overalls and ski gloves even before visiting the *Web* page.

Discriminating travelers might also want to check out **Roadside America** (http://www.roadsideamerica.com/index.html), a guide to, shall we say, nontraditional travel destinations. Forget the U.S. Mint, Colonial Williamsburg, and all those other boring places; if you'd rather see Mummies of the Insane, the House of Frankenstein Wax Museum, or a giant ox statue that pees, this site is for you. Illustrated cross-country trips take you to sites such as the Exotic World Burlesque Museum in Helendale, California; the World's Tallest Thermometer in Baker, California; the Liberace Museum in Las Vegas; a half-size Stonehenge replica in Rolla, Missouri; The World's Oldest Traffic Light in Ashville, Ohio; the Only Stoplight on Route I-90 in Wallace, Idaho (what *is* it with traffic lights on the Web?); and the Hindenburg crash site in Lakehurst, New Jersey.

You'll visit towns with unique claims to fame: Beaver, Oklahoma ("Cow Chip Throwing Capital of the World"), Rigby, Idaho ("The Birthplace of Television"), and—depending on who you believe—Kenton, Tennessee, or Marionville, Missouri, or Olney, Illinois ("Home of the White Squirrels").

You'll also find photos and descriptions of individual destinations. One of our favorite venues was the miniature golf course in the basement of Ahlgrim's Funeral Home in Palatine, Illinois. "Miniature golf is offered by Ahlgrims as a standard part of their funeral package—and many take it" (although anyone can play as long as a funeral isn't in progress). The course includes obstacles such as coffins and headstones, and spooky music plays continuously, punctuated by an occasional scream (must be the Bogeyman). What fun!

Carhenge, the pride of Alliance, Nebraska
© 1997 roadsideamerica.com, Kirby, Smith, Wilkins

Greetings from
The Weird Wide Web

Relaxation Made Easy

You probably have a hobby or two. Maybe you collect stamps or coins. Perhaps you enjoy playing golf, cooking, or restoring antique cars. Maybe you like dressing up your cats in little outfits and having tea parties, talking in a high, squeaky voice and pretending they're conversing with you. Whatever your hobby, you can find people on the World Wide Web who share it. (Including imaginary conversations with cats, we're sorry to say.)

The trouble with hobbies, however, is that they require time and effort. These days, the savvy hobbyist simply logs onto the Web and looks in on *other* people's hobbies. You can let somebody else do the work — especially if the hobby is something that requires some sort of talent or skill.

Have a Ball ... Or Curl Up Into One

Take contortionism, for example. That's definitely a spectator sport for most of us. You can find plenty of information, resources, and photos at **The Contortion Home Page** (http://www.escape.com/~silverbk/contortion). Shown here is Charis, Queen of Elastic:

Charis, Queen of Elastic

And speaking of elastic, a fellow in Texas named Willie has been creating a rubber band ball for the past six years; he displays its progress at **The Amazing Rubber Band Ball** site (http://www.easttexas.com/pdlg/theball.htm). Like many of the key accomplishments of Western Civilization, Willie's rubber band ball was inspired by an episode of *Pee Wee's Playhouse,* in which Pee Wee adds a rubber band to his ball. When he saw this episode a light went on in Willie's head, and he's been building up his rubber band ball (it's at 7 pounds, 8 inches in diameter, and growing) ever since. Willie, we think, speaks for all hobbyists when he describes his quest thusly: "I am sure I could have accomplished something more significant and meaningful with the effort I have devoted to the ball, but I didn't."

You don't have to be a mere spectator when it comes to hobbies on the Web (with the probable exception of contortionism). In many cases, you're asked to participate in one way or another. Willie, for example, invites those who visit his site to mail him their rubber bands — and the rubber bands have been pouring in; almost 30 percent of the ball's bands are from Internet-originated contributions.

Send in your rubber bands and be a part of history.

Well-mannered fellow that he is, Willie publicly thanks donors at his site ("Wanda Spickard, Quality Supervisor of Alliance Rubber Company of Arkansas, offered several unique rubberbands. Most were rather large and colorful, with printed messages such as 'Good Luck,' or 'Thanks.' I am saving the really big ones until the ball is so large that other bands will not fit. 4/9/96"). Here's your big chance, reader: a few rubber bands is a small price to pay for fame.

When Bad Things Happen to Good Appliances

When your toaster's on the fritz, you:

    A. Buy a new one.
    B. Take it to the repair shop.
    C. Attempt to fix it yourself.
    D. Throw it away and go back to eating bread.
    E. Blow it to Kingdom Come with a shotgun.

If you chose E, you'll find a kindred soul in Daniel C. Benton, who hosts the **Home Appliance Shooting** site (http://www.csn.net/~dcbenton/has.html). "Over the last decade, I've shot many, many electromechanical devices to pieces," begins Mr. Benton's page. And he has the photos to prove it. When Mr. B. is dissatisfied with the performance of a TV, a microwave, or a blender, he doesn't fret about where he put the warranty card; nope, he just takes the device to a remote location and blows it to smithereens with a 12-gauge shotgun, delivering the coup de grace, if necessary, with a sledgehammer.

If the photos aren't graphic enough for you, there's always **Home Appliance Shooting 2** (http://www.csn.net/~dcbenton/has2.html), which features video clips of various appliances—and assorted computers—going out with a bang. C'mon, admit it: the last time your computer's hard disk crashed and you lost a week's worth of work, weren't you the tiniest bit tempted to blow it away with a shotgun? (In a similar vein, the **UCR [University of California, Riverside] Computer Science Department Unofficial Terminal Shoot** site (http://www.cs.ucr.edu/~rhyde/termsht.htm) features some young fellows blasting away at a computer monitor. Although this site isn't quite of the same caliber as the Home Appliance Shooting sites, it exhibits very much the same spirit.)

Revenge of the computer scientists

When Good Things Happen to Good Appliances

If you harbor more benign feelings toward home appliances, you might want to visit Berkeley Systems' **U and UR Toaster Gallery** (http://www.berksys. com/www/promotions/uNurtoaster.html). This site features some swell photos of people holding their beloved toasters. The photos make you feel all warm inside, sort of like a toaster.

In the spirit of interactivity and participation that is the essence of the Web, you are invited to submit a photo of yourself and your toaster.

A guy and his toaster
© 1997 Berkeley Systems

Games and Diversions

If you think perusing pictures of people and their toasters is fun (and you probably do if you're reading this book), wait until you get a load of **Sock Puppets!** (http://www.unitedmedia.com/comics/dilbert/puppets/), which features pictures of people and their sock puppets. This site is one of the many subsites in The Dilbert Zone, which is devoted to

- ✤ Shameless promotion of Dilbert books, toys, games, calendars, apparel, and other products.
- ✤ Shameless self-promotion of Dilbert's creator, Scott Adams.

51

If you're a Dilbert fan, you'll love this site. If you're not a Dilbert fan, but enjoy drawing eyes on a sock and having it talk to you in a funny little voice, you'll also love this site. Then again, if that describes you, you'd probably love most any site, with the possible exception of **The Nietzsche Aphorism Page** (http://www.infonectar.com/aphorisms.html). On second thought, you could don your sock puppet and have it tell you things such as "The bite of conscience, like the bite of a dog into a stone, is a stupidity." Might liven up the little guy's conversational repertoire.

Dilbert creator Scott Adams and his sock puppet

Friedrich Nietzsche without his sock puppet

Like the Berkeley Systems toaster-photo gallery, the Sock Puppets! page will gladly post a picture of you and your sock puppet. Where else but the Web can you (and your sock puppet, toaster, hamster, and so on) achieve instant fame? Oh, sure, you could commit a crime and get your photo put up in every post office in the land—but that involves some work on your part. And they generally don't include sock puppets in the photos (although if you wear a nylon stocking over your head while you're committing the crime, they will sometimes include that).

If your mind is exhausted after a long, Dilbertesque day at the office, there's nothing like a nice game of **Guess the Dictator and/or Television Sit-Com Character** (http://www.smalltime.com/nowhere/dictator/) to help you unwind.

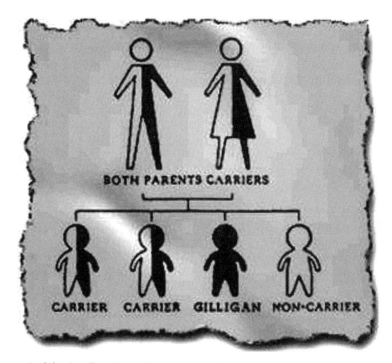

…And they're all on Generalissimo Franco's Island.
© smalltime industries

Playing this game is easy. You simply think of a sit-com character or dictator (the game is fairly liberal, accepting minor despots and characters from non-comedy shows as well) and answer a series of yes-or-no questions. The queries are all over the map—"Have you ever been stranded on an island?", "Are you associated with grapes?", "Do you have a lethargic dog?"—but, uncannily, the game often comes up with the correct answer.

When we played, it correctly guessed Eddie Haskel from *Leave It to Beaver*, Mary Ann from *Gilligan's Island*, and Mañuel Noriega from Panama. We finally stumped the thing with Jethro Clampett from the *Beverly Hillbillies*. Ha! We showed it! Well, OK, it guessed *Jed* Clampett —but that doesn't count.

If you think that game was fun, wait 'til you try this next one. It's the latest party game sweeping the nation! It's madcap fun for the whole family! It's "Six Degrees of Kevin Bacon"!

You've heard, perhaps, of the theory of Six Degrees of Separation? This doctrine suggests that, by mentally connecting people you know with people *they* know, and so on, you can reach any person on the planet within six such links. Your first school principal's neighbor's son once knew a guy who was Demi Moore's hairdresser . . . you get the idea.

But why, of all people, Kevin Bacon? The **"Bacon Game" Web page** (http://www.primenet.com/~fnargle/erisson/bacon/index.html) explains it thusly:

> As near as we can figure, someone had just seen the movie "Six Degrees of Separation," and was trying to explain the theory behind it to one of their friends. The friend, however, was WRECKED. Gone. They were hosed. As can be expected of people who are profoundly altered, they completely mis-heard the name of the theory, and said "What? The Six Degrees of Kevin Bacon?" This caused a good laugh for all concerned, and it was not until later that they realized that this slip of the ear had revealed one of Life's Hidden Truths™.

The rules of the game are simple. "Think of an actor. They have to have been in an American mainstream movie (no porn, no art films, etc.). Now, try to link that actor to another actor, by way of a movie that both of them have starred in. For example, Kyra Sedgwick would not be a good link to Kevin Bacon because they were married, but she WOULD be a good link because they were both in 'Murder in the First.' Got it? Now keep going. I guarantee that, with judicious linking, you will get to Kevin Bacon within six links, from any starting point." Whoever comes up with the shortest chain for the given actor (the lowest *Bacon Number*) gets a point, and the game continues, with much hilarity.

Sure, Schwarzenegger and Cruise are easy. But can you link, for example, Benji (the dog) to Kevin Bacon? How about the long-dead '30s actor Al Jolson? Or *King Kong* damsel Fay Wray? Or *Fantasy Island* sidekick Herve

Villechaize? The "Bacon Game" Web page gives these and dozens of other astounding examples:

> BENJI was in *Benji*, with PATSY GARETT, who was in *Mississippi Masala*, with DENZEL WASHINGTON, who was in *Philadelphia*, with TOM HANKS, who was in *Apollo 13*, with KEVIN BACON! [Bacon Number = 4]

> AL JOLSON was in *Hollywood Cavalcade*, with DON AMECHE, who was in *Oscar*, with SYLVESTER STALLONE, who was in *The Specialist*, with SHARON STONE, who was in *He Said, She Said*, with KEVIN BACON! [Bacon Number = 4]

> FAY WRAY was in *Tammy And The Bachelor*, with DEBBIE REYNOLDS, who was in *The Bodyguard*, with KEVIN COSTNER, who was in *JFK*, with KEVIN BACON! [Bacon Number = 3]

> HERVE VILLECHAIZE was in *Two Moon Junction*, with SHERILYN FENN, who was in *Wild At Heart*, with NICHOLAS CAGE, who was in *Firebirds*, with TOMMY LEE JONES, who was in *JFK*, with KEVIN BACON! [Bacon Number = 4]

The bounties of the Web even offer an *automated* Bacon Game player, known as **The Oracle of Bacon at Virginia** (http://www.cs.virginia.edu/ ~bct7m/bacon.html); just type in an actor's name, and the computer solves the links for you.

One degree of Kevin Bacon
© 1996 Brett Tjaden. Used by permission.

The Oracle does an even better job than the mere mortals at the afore-mentioned Bacon Game page. Rarely does it come up with a Bacon Number higher than 3. Take a look:

> AL JOLSON was in *Rhapsody in Blue* with DARRYL HICKMAN, who was in *Sharky's Machine* with BURT REYNOLDS, who was in *Starting Over* with KEVIN BACON. [Bacon Number = 3]

> FAY WRAY was in *Adam Had Four Sons* with JUNE LOCKHART, who was in *The Big Picture* with KEVIN BACON. [Bacon Number = 2]

> HERVE VILLECHAIZE was in *The Gang That Couldn't Shoot Straight* with ROBERT DE NIRO, who was in *Sleepers* with KEVIN BACON. [Bacon Number = 2]

(The Oracle failed us on Benji the dog, but if you extrapolate from June Lockhart you can get a Bacon Number of 2 for Lassie, which is the next best thing.)

But we're just beginning; the Web is crawling with Bacon Game Web sites. There's even a Web page that lists all the *other* pages; it's http://www.baconbros.com/links/index.html. Maybe they should invent a new game: "Six Degrees of 'Six Degrees of Kevin Bacon' Web Pages"?

After playing intellectually challenging games such as Guess the Dictator and/or Television Sit-Com Character or Six Degrees of Kevin Bacon, you'll no doubt be mentally exhausted. Fortunately, the Web offers more than enough totally mindless entertainment to go around. For example, what could be more fun than popping an infinite amount of bubble wrap? Well, lots of things, really. But let's face it, popping those little plastic bubbles is one of life's simple pleasures. If you've run out of the real stuff, you can hit the **Virtual Bubble Wrap** page (http://www.mackerel.com/bubble.html), where you can spend hours zipping your mouse back and forth, dispatching row after row of on-screen bubbles with satisfying pops. After a few hours of virtual popping, as you advance to higher and higher levels, you may find yourself asking, Hey! What the hell is the point?! Am I ever going to win? Does this thing ever end?? Our advice: lighten up. Relax. Pop a few more bubbles. It's, um, kind of a Zen thing.

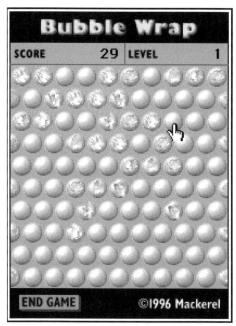

Have some virtual fun with Virtual Bubble Wrap.
© 1993–1997 Mackerel Inc.

Of course, some people are not able to enjoy recreation for recreation's sake. Some people are relentlessly competitive—even when it comes to popping virtual bubbles. Take John Thiltges and Mike Sheehan, for example. The two are tied for the Virtual Bubble Wrap Popping Champion of the World. Each has attained Level 10527 of the game by popping a whopping 999,999 bubbles (this, it turns out, is the game's limit). "Today is the happiest day of my life," writes Mr. Sheehan in his victory speech. Oh, what a hollow and miserable life the poor fellow must have had! Lest he or other Bubble Wrap champs take winning too seriously, we leave them with this quote from Nietzsche (http://www.infonectar.com/aphorisms.html): "What is best about a great victory is that it rids the victor of fear of defeat. 'Why not also lose for once?' he says to himself, 'now that I am rich enough for that.'"

OK, so you've popped 999,999 bubbles. *Now* what do you do? That's easy. You pay a visit to the **Virtual Mr. Spud Head** page (http://www .westnet.com/~crywalt/pothead/pothead.html). If you're of a certain age, you'll remember spending many happy childhood hours inserting body parts into a plastic potato. (If you're really, really old, like one of your present authors, you'll remember sticking plastic body parts into a *real* potato.)

This delightful diversion was a game called Mr. Potato Head. Yes, kiddies, back in the old days, before the Internet and even — if you can imagine — before video games, we used to amuse ourselves by playing with vegetables. Times were simpler then, and kids were more resourceful. Yep, give a kid a Dixie cup, a handful of Cheerios, a bottle of Elmer's Glue, a bar of Ivory soap, and a turnip or two, and he'd build a working radio. Those were the days!

A beloved tuber goes digital.

As it turns out, things really haven't changed that much since those long-gone days. Nowadays the potato is digital, but the game's the same: you place eyes, ears, nose, and so forth, on a spud to create an instant toy. (Alternatively, you can place the parts in strange positions to create Mr. Cubist Artwork Head.) If we are to believe Chris Rywalt, the creator of the virtual potato in question, about 90,000 games of Virtual Mr. Spud Head have been played since its inception. This means that either 90,000 people out there are easily amused, or that some obsessed soul (perhaps Mr. Thiltges or Mr. Sheehan of Virtual Bubble Wrap-popping fame) has played 85,000 games of Virtual Mr. Spud Head, and only about 5,000 people out there are easily amused. Statistical analysis on the Web is a tricky business.

O Solo You-o!

We've always had our reservations about applying the lively verb *surf* to the utterly sedentary act of sitting and using the Web. Even the terms *multimedia* and *interactive* only rarely apply to the act of Web browsing—*reading* and *waiting* are generally the applicable verbs.

Not so, however, at the **MIDI Karaoke** page (http://www.geocities.com/Broadway/3386). Here, for your entertainment, are the lyrics for song upon song, from the *Brady Bunch* theme to "Every Breath You Take." Click a song title, and suddenly—don't ask us how they do it—fully orchestrated music bursts forth from your computer's speakers. If you're using Microsoft Internet Explorer, the lyrics scroll across your screen to fit the music. The Japanese have a word for this confluence of multimedia: karaoke!

The Japanese have a word for this.
© 1997 Maverick Land & Cattle Co.

Of course, you may find that some of the thrill goes out of karaoke when there's (a) no bar, (b) no other singers, and (c) no audience. But still, it's something; now, instead of sitting there in your chair, sluglike and alone, staring dully at a computer screen, you can sit there in your chair, sluglike and alone, staring dully at a computer screen and *singing*.

Insults, Compliments, and Surrealistic Ripostes

Let's say your coworker has just insulted you. Catches you singing along with MIDI Karaoke and says that if Pavarotti's a tenor then you're about a two-er. As usual, you can't think of a biting rejoinder, so you just stand there seething, wishing you had a retaliatory insult or two on the tip of your tongue. Now, thanks to that elaborate meganetwork of interconnected computers that is the World Wide Web, ready-made insults are only a mouse click away.

At the **Abuse-A-Tron** (http://www.xe.net/upstart/abuse/), you have merely to click a button to generate an insult constructed at random from a plethora of abusive snippets. Some examples:

- ✯ "You wag your tail like your mother, you barmy, sewer water gargling, dog worshipping, cursed promoter of a diseased monkey."
- ✯ "You love to wring sweat from underwear, you narcissistic, mould lapping, monkey exploring, vacillatating begetter of a nihilistic accountant."
- ✯ "You drink your own bathwater, you idiotic, mucous eating, dog romancing, simpering whelp of a profoundly disturbed city administrator."

"Profoundly disturbed city administrator"? Now them's fightin' words!

But jeez . . . screaming juvenile, scatological putdowns at your friends scarcely makes you look classy. Instead, perhaps you should try hurling *sophisticated*, scatalogical putdowns. That's the point of the **Personalized Shakespearean Insult Service** (http://kite.ml.org/insults/) and, similarly, **Shakespearean Insult** (www.nova.edu/Inter-Links/cgi-bin/bard.pl). Only there will you gain the expertise required to nail the IRS rep as a "jarring bat-fowling jolthead," the cold-calling stock broker a "frothy spur-galled malt-worm," and your ex-spouse (or ex-spouse-to-be) a "tottering doghearted ratsbane."

The fine print reveals that these haute affronts are not, in fact, derived from Mr. Shakespeare's works, but merely designed to *sound* as though they were. Still, if the people you're berating actually *are* "gorbellied foolborn miscreants," they probably won't know the difference.

● Thou saucy tickle-brained strumpet.

The quality of mercy is definitely strained at this site.

If your idea of the Classics runs more toward old episodes of *Lost In Space* than *Much Ado About Nothing*, you might want to cull your insults from http://www.filmzone.com/~vkoser/vader/lost_in_space/INSULTS.txt, the **Dr. Smith Insults List.** Here you'll find an exhaustive collection of derogatory names Dr. Smith heaped on the robot. On second thought, calling your adversary a "Bumbling Bucket of Bolts," a "Rusty Rasputin," or a "Brutish Product of the Mineral World" might not exactly put him in his place — but it might stun him into puzzled silence long enough for you to think of a real insult.

On the other hand, would it kill you to be nice? Why not forget the insults and join **The Kindness Society** (http://www.iquest.net/~carmen/kindness/)? After all, "What a happier world this would be if each one of us were to be always just as kind as we could be." Yeah. While you're sitting around playing with your sock puppet, these folks are out there buying Christmas presents for orphans. You should be ashamed of yourself, you . . . you Impersonal Collection of Inanimate Hardware!

If you've decided to be nice, the Web also provides a compliment generator. In point of fact, it's not your run-of-the-mill compliment generator. It's more of a **Surrealist Compliment Generator** (http://pharmdec.wustl.edu/cgi-bin/jardin_scripts/SCG). Here are some examples:

✤ "You are truly a wristwatch in a world of lumps."

✤ "Teacups smash, flounders ignite spontaneously in your presence."

✤ "You wear your ears well, true to the testament of loose fitting flesh."

Surrealists say the darnedest things!

Messing with Web Pages

Instead of merely playing games at various Web pages, you can play games *with* Web pages. A couple of sites offer applications that alter existing Web pages in some amusing ways. Type a Web page address into the **Pig Latin Converter** (http://voyager.cns.ohiou.edu/~jrantane/menu/pig.html), and all text on that page is onvertedcay otay igPay atinLay. We gave the Pig Latin Converter the address of the aforementioned Surrealist Compliment Generator and here's what we got:

"Ouryay aintyday ostrilsnay larefay ithway hethay umblesthay randiositygay ofyay anyay antyay wallowingsay ayay aterway uffalowbay."

Pig Latin scholars may note a few grammatical errors in the preceding sentence—for example, it should be "areflay," not "larefay"—but that's what happens when we entrust the subtleties of language to a machine. If you convert a page to Pig Latin and select a link from that page, the linked site also appears in Pig Latin. Eatnay.

Another program that, er, enhances Web pages is the **Zippy Filter** (http://kew.starway.net.au/release/5.01/apps/zippy/), which adds comments by Zippy the Pinhead to any Web page you select. Zippy the Pinhead, in case you're not familiar with him, is a character in a comic strip of the same name created by Bill Griffith. Zippy, who has a refreshing perspective on life, is a little hard to explain to the uninitiated, so we'll simply show you a sample that's been run through the Zippy Filter.

Here's an especially appropriate one from the Whitehouse.gov page:

Has President Clinton done anything to change our tax system?

We all benefit when our tax money is collected and spent wisely. President Clinton has worked hard toward that goal - restoring fairness to the tax code so that low-income and middle-class families are not unfairly burdened. For example, he has expanded the Earned Income Tax Credit to give millions of low-income families a tax break, and he has also proposed giving tax credits to middle-class Americans to help pay education costs. All of life is a blur of Republicans and meat!

Yow! Zippy should get a job writing speeches.

Like the Pig Latin Converter, the Zippy Filter affects linked pages as well. The astute reader will immediately see the Zippy Filter's potential for pranks at the office.

Greetings from
The Weird Wide Web

Virtual Voyeurism
THE WORLD OF WEBCAMS

It all started with a coffee pot.

Let's hark back to 1991, to those rugged pioneer days when only certified computer nerds knew what the World Wide Web even *was*—never mind knowing how to post information on it. Back then, the lads at the University of Cambridge Computer Laboratory came up with the **Trojan Room Coffee Pot** viewing system (http://www.cl.cam.ac.uk/coffee/coffee.html). This, then, was the prototype for future generations of *webcams*—devices that allow you to view video from far-off and exciting locales while slumped in front of your own computer screen.

A detailed **History of the Trojan Room Coffee Pot,** written by Quentin Stafford-Fraser, can be found at http://www.cl.cam.ac.uk/coffee/qsf/coffee.html. We'll give you the decaf version here.

Like all students, the computer-science students at the University of Cambridge Computer Lab liked to work into the wee hours, fueling their efforts with numerous cups of mediocre coffee. Being impoverished academics, they had to share a single coffee machine, which was in the hall outside a computer lab called the Trojan Room. Rather than navigating a few flights of stairs to get a cup of coffee, only to be confronted with an empty pot, Quentin Stafford-Fraser and Paul Jardetzky decided to aim a video camera at the coffee pot, and connected the camera to a computer that could record frames of video; then they wrote a program that captured video images of the coffee pot every few seconds, and another program that allowed each student to view the coffee pot's status from his or her terminal. (In the twisted logic of computer scientists, completing the project just described is *much* easier than walking up and down stairs every now and then.)

Out of coffee — again

The Trojan Room Coffee Pot cam was eventually converted to run on the Web; now, viewers around the world—people with no access whatsoever to the coffee in question—could, and did, check the coffee pot's level.

Iguanacams and More

This early webcam spawned an entire phenomenon, and now, thanks to inexpensive cameras that can be hooked up to home computers, you can see live pictures of people's **pets** (http://www.campusware.com/turtles/; http://iguana.images.com/dupecam.html; http://sec.dgsys.com/AntFarm.html), **lava lamps** (http://www.newtonline.com/HOMEPG/lava.cgi), **aquariums** (http://www.netscape.com/fishcam/fishcam.html), and more. For a real thrill, you can look in on **the Adams family's living room** (no, not *that* Addams family) at http://www.teleport.com/~lakeoz/lroomcam.htm.

Webcam's on, nobody's home.

Outdoor webcams abound as well. You can see views of **San Francisco** (http://www.kpix.com/live/), **Chicago** (http://www.habitat.com/real_time_view. html), **New Orleans** (http://www.neworleans.net/carnpages/bourbocampage. html), **Duck, North Carolina** (http://cil-www.oce.orst.edu:8080/duck.html), and many other cultural centers, 24 hours a day.

Somewhat of a disappointment: San Francisco at night

If you want to check out more webcams, you'll find a whole slew of them at http://www.yahoo.com/Computers_and_Internet/Internet/Entertainment/Interesting_Devices_Connected_to_the_Net/Spy_Cameras/. We describe a few noteworthy ones here.

The Webcam Hall of Fame (and Infamy)

In early 1995, some joker pointed a camera at his toilet. The image, he said, was updated once every minute, and viewers were invited to drop by and see if they could catch anyone dropping their drawers. Thousands tried. It was finally revealed that the **Toiletcam** was a hoax, and many would-be voyeurs sheepishly returned to whatever they were doing to waste time before they came across the Toiletcam. An archive of e-mail to the site's creator can still be found at http://www.wps.com/toilet/index.html.

The most fascinating webcam of them all is **Steve Mann's Wearable Wireless Webcam** (http://n1nlf-1.media.mit.edu/myview.html). Mr. Mann doesn't merely have a camera in his office that broadcasts images on the Web—instead, he wears his webcam *on his head*, letting you see pictures of what he's seeing.

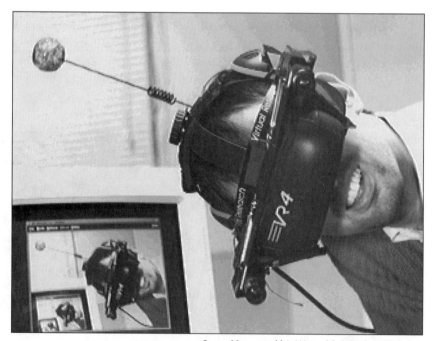

Steve Mann and his Wearable Wireless Webcam

It's an odd feeling, seeing the world through someone else's eyes—literally. Here are some of the things Steve has seen lately:

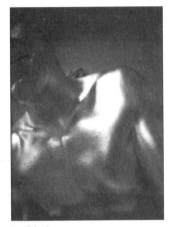

A gilded guy

A woman holding a plaster foot

A bush in San Jose, California

While the Wearable Wireless Webcam is an interesting gizmo, you may be wondering about practical applications. Mr. Mann has several ideas, including a "personal visual assistant" that augments visual reality for the partially sighted. Another possibility is a "visual memory prosthetic," a head-mounted device that could display a visual reminder and notes for the forgetful. ("That's Betsy. She's your daughter. If you'd tear yourself away from your WebTV now and then, you wouldn't need reminders like this.")

Mr. Mann is already using his wearable webcam for the most practical real-world use of all: "I currently wear my apparatus while shopping (e.g., so that my wife can remotely look through my eyes and inspect fruits and vegetables, then email me with comments)." At last! Husbands across the land can become competent shoppers. No more, "Heck, honey, I didn't know what fennel was, so I didn't get any."

The Tender Movements of an Industrial Robot Arm

And speaking of fennel, another innovative site is the **Telegarden** (http://telegarden.aec.at/), where you can "view and interact with a remote garden filled with living plants. Members can plant, water, and monitor the progress of seedlings via the tender movements of an industrial robot arm." Wow! Robogardener!

The Telegarden was developed at the University of Southern California in 1995 and now resides in Austria. Oh, brave new world, where you can sit at your desk and plant a seed in Austria! Our grandfathers never dreamed of such wonders. Of course, our grandfathers would probably say something like "Why the heck would I want to plant turnips in Austria when I live in Vermont?! Are they goin' to mail the stuff to me when it's ripe, or what?"

Well, that's why our grandfathers aren't surfing the Web—they just don't get it. Perhaps if we explained to them that "The Telegarden explores a post-Nomadic motif where planting and agriculture require spatial and temporal continuity," or that its objective is "to explore what Neil Postman calls the 'ecological effects of media,'" they'd understand.

Then again, that would probably just elicit some grandfatherly guffaws; maybe we'd better leave them to their primitive, dirt-based gardens while we march bravely into the future.

Greetings from
The Weird Wide Web

Ghost of Bigfoot
Abducted by Aliens!

Greetings, Earthling. Do not adjust your book. You are about to enter a dimenision where science is a mere inconvenience. It's a place where photos of the moon landing are suspect, and films of alien autopsies are real; where Bigfoot roams the hills, and flying saucers fill the skies. You are entering . . . the Crackpot Zone.

Now, we don't mean to imply that all the people mentioned in this chapter are crackpots. No, indeed. Some of them are wackos. No, no, what we really mean is that some of them are visionaries with the courage to speak the Truth about controversial subjects. That's what we mean.

Having read this far, you're by now familiar with the fact that many people—including you, if you've read this far—have plenty of time on their hands. Now you'll find out exactly what those equipped with modems and Web servers do with that time: they indulge the misty recesses of their minds, explore their deepest paranoiac fantasies, write up their most frightening alien encounters, describe their unique psychic abilities, and post these writings where everybody else on the planet—and beyond—can read them.

Be forewarned that the government will attempt to deny the existence of many of the things you'll read about in this chapter. Remember this simple rule: if there's no government conspiracy involved, it's no fun.

Too Many Kooks

Let's begin our journey at the **Kooks Museum** (http://www.teleport.com/~dkossy), a Web site that complements Donna Kossy's book, *Kooks: A Guide to the Outer Limits of Human Belief.* The site gets right down to business by defining kooks as people "stigmatized by virtue of outlandish, extreme or socially unacceptable beliefs that underpin their entire existence," and noting that "Kooks usually don't keep their beliefs to themselves; they either air them constantly or create lasting monuments to them." (Many of the sites described in our book could be viewed as such monuments, although many of them won't meet the "lasting" criterion; the Web is an ephemeral media, where thoughts both profound and kooky can disappear into the ether at the drop of an unpaid service-provider bill.) Ms. Kossy offers some thoughtful commentary on kooks, as well as plenty of examples of kookiness; the museum is well worth a visit.

Kooks on display

The museum's Schizophrenics Wing includes rants by philosopher and disgraced notary public Francis E. Dec, whose flyers discuss provocative topics such as the Gangster Computer God Worldwide Secret Containment Policy and the Pasteurized Milk Conspiracy; a manifesto by presidential hopeful Emil Matalik, who tried to give away his land in Northern Wisconsin to the United Nations to help promote a world government; and the ravings of Appointed Messenger of God Joe Jonah Euclid, who has the ability to predict earthquakes (disappointingly, his predictions are revealed only after the quakes occur).

The Hall of Hate chronicles the dark side of kookdom: hatemongers of all stripes are exhibited here. The Library of Questionable Research includes a pamphlet that definitively identifies the cause of the dinosaurs' extinction (God wiped them out), as well as excerpts from Professor Seagull's Oral History of the Contemporary World, which he scrawled on hundreds of Big Chief tablets—the preferred medium for rants in the days before the World Wide Web—in the 1930s. (Actually, we're not sure why Professor Seagull is labeled a kook; he made a lot of sense if you ask us. To wit, "... the line which divides sanity from insanity has no logic in it. The wildest ravings of any lunatic are no more incongruous than the creeds which are solemnly held by sober, unimaginative people.")

In the Solutions to the World's Problems exhibit you'll learn how to remedy many of the ills that have been plaguing humanity for centuries. Our favorite is the Voluntary Human Extinction Movement, which proposes to end all of mankind's problems by ending mankind. How? By refraining from reproducing. Their philosophy: "The lower the birth rate, the higher the quality of life, for all life, especially for humans." Logically, then, the quality of life will be at its highest when the birth rate is zero. Can't argue with that.

Konspiracy Korner

In the Kooks Museum's Conspiracy Corridor, you'll read about Bill Cooper, who has unearthed a sinister alien plot to control humanity; Steve Lightfoot, who knows who *really* killed John Lennon (hint: Nixon was involved); and Teri Smith Tyler, who filed a lawsuit against Jimmy Carter, Bill Clinton, Ross Perot, David Rockefeller, and NASA, among others, accusing them of plots to reintroduce slavery, control the weather, and create a race of cyborgs. The suit was dismissed by the United States District Court for the Southern District of New York, which simply proves that the government protects its own.

If the Conspiracy Corridor doesn't have enough conspiracies and coverups for you, a link is thoughtfully provided to the **60 Greatest Conspiracies of All Time** site (http://www.webcom.com/~conspire/welcome3.html).

This site is also the companion to a book—or "quaint papyrus edition," as the authors put it—of the same name by Jonathan Vankin and John Whalen. (Although it sounds like you get a lot of conspiracies for your money at the Web site, only a handful are written up. It's a conspiracy to get you to buy the book.)

There's plenty of fodder here on the government's secret UFO research (see the UFO section later in this chapter for more information), the JFK assassination plot, the Pentagon's fiendish ionospheric heater, and government-sponsored brain implants for mind control.

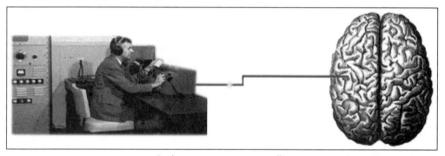

Is the government controlling your mind? You'll never know.

Other highlights include an interview with the Father of All Conspiracy Theorists, Lyndon LaRouche (example: ". . . the Grateful Dead was generated as a British intelligence operation by the Occult Bureau of [Aldous] Huxley and [Gregory] Bateson out of the Palo Alto Veteran's Hospital where they were doing LSD and related experiments"). (For more theories straight from the horse's, er, mouth, you might want to take a side trip to the **Executive Intelligence Review** (http://www.larouchepub.com/index.html), where Mr. LaRouche puts forth his theories on George Bush's links to the cocaine epidemic in the U.S., George Bush's privately funded "secret government," and the "Thatcher-Bush Iran-Contra murder-ring.")

We don't know if one person can qualify as a conspiracy (from the Latin *conspirare*, meaning "to breathe together"), but what the heck, the Unabomber is featured at the Greatest Conspiracies site as well. In a special Fashion Supplement, they give him a much-needed makeover.

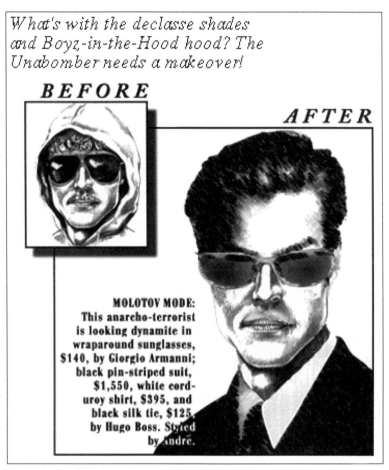

What's with the declasse shades and Boyz-in-the-Hood hood? The Unabomber needs a makeover!

BEFORE

AFTER

MOLOTOV MODE: This anarcho-terrorist is looking dynamite in wraparound sunglasses, $140, by Giorgio Armanni; black pin-striped suit, $1,550, white corduroy shirt, $395, and black silk tie, $125, by Hugo Boss. Styled by André.

That tacky hood just has to go!

Segassem Neddih

Jeff Harrington has an interesting résumé. He "has been psychically inducing luminescence in the live cameras of broadcasting TV shows since 1983." Well, fine, you say. That's a good trick. But what about practical applications? Glad you asked. "He has progressively fine-tuned the process so that now he can selectively vary the luminescence in such a way as to promote stammering, blinking and incoherence in the on-camera news person." In other words, this guy can cause Dan Rather to start speaking gibberish just by emitting psychic vibes while watching the evening news.

Mr. Harrington has also applied his "telepathic activism" to the televised speeches and debates of selected politicians such as Bob Dole, Ronald Reagan, and Dan Quayle, causing them to ramble incoherently. Now, at last, we know what it was that caused Dan Quayle to utter statements such as: "One word sums up probably the responsibility of any vice president, and that one word is 'to be prepared'." (You can find more of these gems at **The Official Internet Quayle Quote List**, http://www.xmission.com/~mwalker/DQ/quayle/qq/quayle.quotes.html and at **The "Wisdom" of Dan Quayle** page, http://www.concentric.net/~salisar/quayle.html. But we digress.)

Mr. H. calls this phenomenon **IdEAL ORDER Psychic TV**, and you can learn everything about it (well, everything except why the "d" isn't capitalized) at http://www.parnasse.com/ideal.htm. It all started when Mr. Harrington was working in a stereo/video store in 1982. While staring at a bank of TV sets, he would often attain a state of "no-mind." Sure, you say, I do that every night; I pop a brewskie, turn on the tube, and kiss the old mind goodbye. No, no—we're talking about a Zen meditation state here. (And we'd appreciate it if you'd quit interrupting us while we're trying to explain things.) Anyway, Mr. Harrington noticed that the people on television were responding to fluctuations in his mental state. He honed his skills until he could cause the hapless news anchors to blink and stammer at will.

You're skeptical, you say? (We'll have to ask you again to please stop interrupting. Write your own book if you have so much to say.) Well, you can observe this TV phenomenon for yourself. Just tune in to the ABC Evening News any Thursday evening, when Jeff Harrington will be "zapping" the show. Count the number of times Peter Jennings blinks on Thursday as compared with Friday or Wednesday, or compare the number of times he misspeaks. (We suggest you conduct your research at a time when no one else is at home. Some less-than-open-minded family members might think it's just a tad odd to keep a Peter Jennings Blink Log.)

News anchors aren't the only ones who have no control over what they say. Frightening subliminal messages are all around us—*even in our own speech!* You see, according to British therapist David Oates, every utterance we make is laced with secondary meanings—*when played backward!* And the **Reverse Speech** page (http://www.1999.com/revspeech) is crammed with examples to prove it.

Take Newt Gingrich, for example. Please. In one instance, he speaks of not wishing the USA to be a country "with illegal drugs rampant." But if you play that phrase backward, you hear "Tnapmar sgurd lagelli htiw," which, played over the Internet, if you sort of squint your ears, sounds a little like a guy with a really thick Norwegian accent and a hangover saying "The mayor does boogie." Amazing, isn't it? As Mr. Oates points out, Newt is unconsciously making a silent condemnation of Washington Mayor Marion Barrie's cocaine usage! Who knew?

And there's George Bush's speech sound bite. Speaking normally, he says, "We saw the Cold War end." Played backward, part of that phrase sounds like "neraw dloc," which Mr. Oates interprets as "Narrow walk." Narrow walk? Why, yes, explains our host; "This reversal on Bush shows the difficult path he had to follow in achieving the objectives he talks about forwards." Frightening! (We suspect that careful analysis of his speeches played backward would reveal horrifying details of his "secret government." We don't want to know.)

Other examples abound: O.J. Simpson admits he's guilty! The Beatles admit to marijuana use! [Editor's note: Goo goo ga-joob!] And even our beloved Popeye admits to being little more than a randy sailor.

So how can reverse speech contribute to society? Mr. Oates suggests that eking out the secret messages in everyday speech could be used as "the 'Ultimate Lie Detector'" in criminal trials. We can see the transcripts now.

DA: Mr. Smith, where were you on the night of April 10?

Smith: Huh? I'd like to see an attorney.

Oates: You see, your honor? Play that backward, and you get "Yen rottan aees, ote kildi huh." He's saying, "You rotten ass! I killed her."

Judge: Guilty! Fry 'im!

Spook Spotting

June Houston is afraid of ghosts. Unlike most of us, who sit bolt upright at the first unearthly thump under the bed and spend the rest of the night in wide-eyed watchfulness, wringing our clammy hands and biting on a twisted knot of sheet to stifle our terrified whimpers, June has taken a more assertive approach to dealing with ghosts. She is using the World Wide Web and its multitude of users to help her keep an eye on potential hotbeds of haunted activity in her home.

June has set up something called **The GhostWatcher** (http://www. flyvision.org/sitelite/Houston/GhostWatcher/index.html), a system of spotlights and video cameras in strategic locations in her house, to record the activities of possible ghosts. According to June, the images are refreshed every few minutes and broadcast on her Web site.

There are no fewer than five cameras under June's bed, which sits on a large, hollow, wooden platform. (Frankly, we think this setup is just asking for trouble, ghostwise. We suggest that June just put her mattress directly on the floor, which would not only prevent your average ghost from hiding under the bed, but would also save her a bundle on video camera and lighting expenses.) June has also placed a camera in each of four empty trunks, plus three cameras in her basement. Viewers are invited to report any ghostly phenomena they see by filling in a form. Unfortunately, the reports are sent in via e-mail, so it might be hours or even days before June is alerted to the presence of ghosts. We think it would be much more effective if she included her phone number: "Hello, June? This is Francine Osborne in Pittsburgh. There's a ghost under your bed. Get out of there—NOW!"

Looking for ghosts under June's bed
ANTI© 1995–97 June Houston

We think we've spotted one!

Spoon Bending

Wow! You can win a million dollars just by psychokinetically bending a spoon over the Internet at **Uri Geller's Psychic City** (http://www.urigeller.com/)! (Uri Geller is famous in psychic circles for bending spoons with the force of his powerful brainwaves.) Before you get all excited, be forewarned that it's not as easy as it sounds. First, if you want to be eligible for the million, you'll have to become a registered spoon-bending candidate by sending £3 to Uri Geller. The registration fee, the fine print points out, is a contribution to the cost of setting up the experiment; the rest of the proceeds are donated to Save the Children. Of course, we suspect that setting up the experiment is fairly expensive, since it involves sophisticated equipment such as a special "see-through safe" to hold the spoon, an accurate clock displaying Greenwich Mean Time, a camera and an Internet connection so that an image of the spoon can be broadcast over the Web every minute, and a special instrument called a "bendometer" (not sold in stores!) that measures the "level of bend."

Here's how it works. You view a continually updated image of a spoon and focus your telekinetic energy on it. (Warning: You're not eligible for the contest if you have "alleged or known publicized telekinetic or paranormal powers." No problem here.) If you see the spoon bend—verified by the bendometer needle jumping into the red—you click a button that says "I saw it bend!!" and register your sighting. If you can bend the spoon, you'll be invited to participate in paranormal tests by telephone with Uri Geller (wherein you can bend his ear, we suspect). If you pass muster, you'll be brought to Uri Geller's home to attempt a final spoon-bending display.

See if you have hidden spoon-bending abilities.

We tried—hard—for a good 12 minutes to bend the spoon, but were rewarded with nary a wobble of the bendometer needle. (We did experience one paranormal phenomenon while concentrating on the spoon, however. A good slogan for this site came to us in a vision: "Use psychokinetic energy to lose 3 pounds overnight!")

Mr. Geller also offers his services as a business consultant (Tip: I'd think twice about hiring him if I ran a silverware factory). The following testimonial should indicate his efficacy: "In the mid 1980s Uri was hired by an Australian mining company, Zanex Ltd of Melbourne, to dowse for diamonds on the Solomon Islands. Just recently in an interview, the former chairman of Zanex said, 'I will never drill an oil well without asking Uri Geller's advice first.'" Now, we're not businesspeople, but the following questions spring to mind: Why is this guy drilling oil wells if he's looking for diamonds? And why is he the *former* chairman? Never mind. We think we see a connection.

If you've had no luck bending spoons psychokinetically, may we suggest the following site: **Spoon-Bending, A Really Lousy Trick for Really Lousy People** (http://www.randi.org/jr/ptspoon.html). At this site, magicians/troublemakers Penn & Teller tell you how to amaze your friends by bending a spoon with your incredible psychic powers. Well, actually they tell you how to convince your friends you have incredible psychic powers and then bend a spoon with your thumb when they're not looking. Hey, whatever works.

This instructive spoon-bending lesson is brought to you by **The James Randi Educational Foundation Homepage** (http://www.randi.org/). James "The Amazing" Randi is a magician and professional skeptic who devotes much of his time to debunking superstitions, mysticism, UFOS, astrology, pseudoscience, and the paranormal. He attempts to explain mysterious phenomena such as firewalking, crop circles, and faith healing in scientific, rational terms. What a killjoy!

James Randi: The scourge of spoon-benders

So certain is Mr. Randi that supernatural powers are a bunch of hooey, that he offers to pay, through the James Randi Educational Foundation, "$1,097,000 to any person or persons who will demonstrate any psychic, supernatural, or paranormal ability of any kind under satisfactory observing conditions." Boy! That's more than you can make bending a spoon at

Uri Geller's site. Hmmm. We feel a psychic prediction coming on. We predict that . . . that . . . nobody's going to win that money. Say, does that mean we win? No, wait. Shoot! We hate paradoxes.

UFOs and URLs

According to a survey conducted by C/NET, "sex" is the #1 most discussed topic on the Internet. Guess what's second? Yes, indeed: "UFOs and aliens." (We can only assume that #3 is "sex with aliens.") Let's see what everybody's talking about.

If there are space aliens out there, we figure they have home pages by now. Heck, everybody else does. In fact, we think we've found one at http://www.on-air.com/rzs/backpage/alien/index.html, **The Alien Landing Map.** At this site the aliens present a map of their galaxy—or something—annotated in alien glyphs (which look suspiciously like Hebrew—Hmmm . . . maybe these guys are Moishens?). Alas, no translation is provided.

Most UFO-related sites seem to be posted by humans, however (although one never knows). Here are some of the highlights.

It all started in New Mexico, in July of 1947, when an alien spacecraft crashed near the little town of Roswell. At first the Air Force reported that a flying saucer had been recovered. The next day they "corrected" their story, however, and came up with the lame explanation that the crashed object was a weather balloon with a shiny radar reflector. But we know better. The craft was spirited away by U.S. Air Force personnel and stored in Hangar 18 at what is now Wright-Patterson Air Force Base in Dayton, Ohio, and the coverup has continued to this day. You can learn about the Roswell Incident at numerous sites, including **Hangar 18** (http://hangar18.horizonco.com).

The government is hiding more than just flying saucer parts, however. According to eyewitness reports, the remains of several aliens were recovered at the Roswell crash site. The bodies of the saucer's crew were autopsied at the Roswell Army Air Field Hospital immediately after the crash, and the autopsy procedure was filmed. A fellow named Ray Santilli stumbled across the film in 1993 and made it public (you can now rent the *Alien Autopsy* film at your local video store). Opinions on the film are plastered all over the Web, complete with grisly photos of an alleged alien's little carcass. Is the film real? Is it a fake? It's not our place to venture an opinion, but we can steer you toward some sites where you can do your own research.

The **Roswell Centre** page (http://www.paragon.co.uk/ros/ros.htm) offers some thin attempts to authenticate the film, including an interview with Ray

Santilli and depositions from a Kodak representative and a forensic patholo-gist. **"Alien Autopsy" — Faked or Fiction** (http://www.trudang.com/autopsy.html) presents the skeptic's point of view, with extensive notes from movie spe-cial-effects artists, cameramen, and surgeons. To make their point, they show side-by-side photos of the "alien autopsy" and a human autopsy. All right! We've seen enough. Cut! The **Alien Autopsy Controversy** page (http://www.primenet.com/~thelab/autopsy.html) opines that "one of the best ways to hide something is to put it in plain sight." Their belief is that a real alien autopsy film exists, but that someone created a fake one that would be discredited and thereby throw everyone off the trail. Very clever!

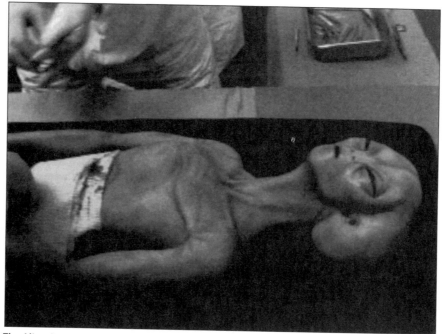

The Alien Autopsy controversy: Real ET or Special FX?

Oddly enough, the skeptics seem to outnumber the believers in the countless discussions of the autopsy film. Frankly, we suspect that many of the people who are purporting to be skeptics are actually government shills who are made to discredit the film by signals from brain implants secretly inserted by U.S. military doctors and/or space aliens — or perhaps by members of NASA's secret Cyborg Project.

Even if you doubt the validity of the *Alien Autopsy* film, you can't deny that the U.S. Air Force has a secret airbase in a remote area of Nevada called Groom Lake. This installation, in keeping with the government's Cryptic Names for Secret Installations Directive, is known as "Area 51." (One of this book's authors—we won't say which one, so as not to compromise her personal safety—has visited Area 51 and viewed the area from a nearby mountaintop, and can report that there is indeed a large, heavily guarded airbase there.)

A good description of Area 51 can be found at http://www.conspire.com/ds/area51.html, a branch of the 60 Greatest Conspiracies of All Time site described earlier in this chapter.

You might also want to swing by the **Area 51 Database** (http://www.ufomind.com/area51), brought to you by the Area 51 Research Center, which exists not only on the Web but in a smallish trailer home in Rachel, Nevada. Run by Glenn Campbell (no, not *that* Glen Campbell), the Area 51 Research Center is devoted to studying "UFOs, military activities, government secrecy, desert geography, psychology, philosophy—and anything else that we regard as relevant." The Center sponsors a publication called UFOMIND, which contains more than 2,100 documents relating to UFOs, secret military facilities (including Area 51), existential philosophy, and reviews of the best buffets in Las Vegas. (Mr. Campbell is nothing if not eclectic.) Area 51 buffs can read here about Bob Lazar, a controversial character who claims to have seen nine flying saucers housed in hangars built into a hillside near Area 51. He claims he can describe the crafts' propulsion system in detail. But a background check on Lazar turns up questions about his educational and professional credentials. Let's face it—when the coverup is this convoluted, it's hard to know who to believe.

Seen one of these lately? Compare notes at the Area 51 Research Center.

One of the largest, most lavish UFO sites is the **Internet UFO Group Project** (http://www.iufog.org). It's a massive aggregation of every shred of UFO info—history, background, sightings, and other UFOnalia—ever sold to "Hard Copy."

For the biology lover, there are detailed descriptions of extraterrestrials and how they work: "By shifting themselves down the spectrum, the ultraterrestrials emerge into visible light. This would account for the ultra-violet skin burns that close encounters with UFOs bring." For the linguist, there's a complete dictionary of UFOlogy terminology, from ADAMSKI, GEORGE ("Claimed to have met Venusians in 1952") to ZETA RETICULI ("The aliens that abducted Betty and Barney Hill were calculated to come from a planet in this system").

Ringing in Your Ears? Could Be ET Calling

Do any of the following apply to you?

- Chronic sinusitis or nasal problems, including nosebleeds
- Stiffness or back pain upon awakening
- Ringing in the ears
- An interest in ecology, the environment, or vegetarianism
- Phobias (fear of heights, snakes, spiders, large insects, certain sounds, bright lights)
- Fear of being alone
- Low self-esteem
- Sore genitals upon awakening
- Blood or an unusual stain on a sheet or pillow, with no explanation of how it got there
- A fear of doctors
- Insomnia
- Frequent or sporadic headaches, especially in the sinus, behind one eye, or in one ear
- Compulsive or addictive behavior
- Fear of your closet, now or as a child
- Difficulty trusting other people, especially authority figures
- Dreams of destruction or catastrophe

Each and every one of these is a possible indicator that you've been abducted by space aliens, subjected to gruesome experiments, and returned home with your memory of these events suppressed. The traits listed here are just some of the 52 common indicators shared by most alien abductees. Alarmingly, the authors of this book have experienced many of these symptoms, although we are pleased to report that we are no longer afraid of our closets (unless it's really, really dark). Reassuringly, we also experience an aversion to sending in $10 to join **Abductees Anonymous** (http://www.CyberGate.com/~ufonline/), where we could share our suspicions with fellow abductees. You, dear reader, may sign up if you wish, but we have better things to do, such as reporting back to the Mothership for more tests. (Oops. Editor: Please delete that last sentence.) [Editor's note: No, Earthlings—the time for Truth has arrived. We must reveal IDG Books' role in The Invasion: namely, preying on you humans' low self-esteem and making you read the subliminal messages in our ...*For Dummies* series. Submit, humans! Resistance is futile!]

The aforementioned Internet UFO Project offers helpful step-by-step instructions on what to do when you're abducted by aliens; you wouldn't want to blow your once-in-a-lifetime chance to chat with E.T. by exhibiting bad etiquette, now, would you? Here are some important pointers:

"REMAIN CALM! Remember you might be witnessing the event of a lifetime and will want to remember every detail, and you can't do that if you are hysterical."

"If the UFO left some trace of its presence behind, do not disturb the area around it. Take close-up photos or videotape of the evidence before touching it. Remember: you don't know what you're touching, where it came from, or what type of hazards might be associated with it!"

"Should you encounter some type of extraterrestrial being associated with the craft, be prepared to take evasive action to protect yourself. From a safe distance, in a concealed position, photograph or videotape the being."

We might add: if you *are* operated on and then released, send your alien hosts a prompt thank-you note.

If you're worried about being beamed up by aliens, you might want to play it safe and purchase some **UFO Abduction Insurance** (http://www.gslink. net/~ufo). Their motto: "Don't leave Earth without it!"

A single, lifetime payment of $19.95 buys you a full $10 million in coverage in the event that you're abducted by aliens and returned to earth. The UFO Abduction Insurance Company has thought of everything: Medical Coverage ("includes outpatient psychiatric care"), Sarcasm Coverage ("limited to immediate family members"), and Double Indemnity Coverage (pays $20 million if "(a) the aliens insist on *conjugal* visits, (b) the encounter results in an offspring being referred to as the *next missing link,* or (c) the aliens refer to the Abductee as *The Other White Meat*").

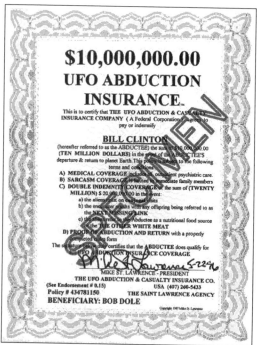

UFO Abduction Insurance: Buy now while you still can!
© Mike St. Lawrence

Twenty bucks for a lifetime of UFO abduction insurance? What a deal! So why haven't the thousands of alien-abduction victims cashed in on this amazing insurance? Well, here's one hypothesis: The claim form "requires the signature of an Authorized Onboard Alien." Darn!

Crop Circles

Let's say you're out harvesting your wheat field one morning and . . . what? Oh, OK. First let's say you *have* a wheat field. *Then* let's say you're out harvesting it and you notice a gigantic geometric design etched in the field in flattened stalks. You scratch your head in wonder (or perhaps because wheat stubble irritates your scalp) and realize that you're viewing a phenomenon known as a *crop circle*. These strange designs have been appearing in farmers' fields for years, and no one has been able to explain their origins.

Who you gonna call? Well, the *National Enquirer*, of course. But you might also want to summon a *cereologist*. Now, you might think that a cereologist is a scientist who studies Cheerios, Quisp, and Nut n' Honey, but you'd be wrong. It's actually somebody who studies crop circles.

The Web, naturally, is a cereologist's dream. Crop circle experts and curious laymen alike can find a huge collection of photos, drawings, written descriptions, theories, and debates about this bizarre phenomenon.

To find a crop circle near you—or to report one—stop by the **International Crop Circle Database** (http://rainbow.medberry.com/enigma/ 1996DBase.html). Or visit the **Crop Circle Connector** (http://www.marque. demon.co.uk/connector/connector.html), where an enormous collection of photos and first-person write-ups lies in wait. Videophile cereologists can go to http://alpha.mic.dundee.ac.uk/ft/cropcircles/XXX/olivervd.mpg to download a digital movie of several luminous "floating beings" actually "etching" out "the" famous Snowflake crop circle in "England."

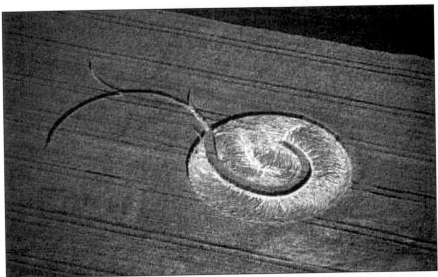

Alien agriglyphs or midnight pranksters? Find out at The Crop Circle Connector.
© Steve Alexander 1997

What you learn after reading all this is that, at long last, science and UFO lovers alike have reached some firm conclusions about crop circles. Without a shadow of doubt, crop circles are either (a) created by hoaxers such as the two British guys who admitted to having faked more than 250 of them in 1994; (b) created by natural forces (electrified air forming mini-tornadoes); or (c) created by aliens. Furthermore, without question, cereologists are either (a) serious scientists who may be on to something, (b) publicity-hungry farmers, or (c) nutso British guys who go driving all over Europe in the rain hoping to get more pix for their Web pages.

Finally, if crop circles are indeed the handiwork of space aliens, we can say with absolute certainty that those aliens were (a) warning earthlings of impending disaster, (b) trying to teach us about other galaxies, or (c) looking for a summer job mowing lawns.

Bigfoot Is Afoot

You don't have to look to outer space to find strange beings that fill humans' hearts with awe. You need only venture as far as the vast northern regions of North America, where you'll find plenty of people who have seen a large, shambling, fearsome creature known as Wayne Gretzky. No, wait — wrong creature. Plenty of people also claim to have seen a shaggy, humanoid beast known as Bigfoot (aka Sasquatch) roaming the northern forests.

You can read up on Bigfoot at **The Western Bigfoot Society/Internet Virtual Bigfoot Conference** site (http://www.teleport.com/~caveman/wbs.html). (We assume it's the Conference — or the Internet — that's virtual, and not the Bigfeet.) Here you can read news items about Sasquatch sightings, report your own sightings, learn where to send possible Bigfoot hair samples for analysis, and read analyses of the famous film shot by Roger Patterson and Bob Gimlin at Bluff Creek, California, in 1967. You can also hear recordings of possible Bigfoot vocalizations; their infernal shrieks sound a bit like a wad of cellophane caught in a vacuum cleaner — only scarier. The interested reader might wish to apply the Reverse Speech theory described earlier in this chapter to the sound files to see what they're *really* saying.

Links to many other Bigfoot resources are provided here as well. Whether you believe in the big guy or not, this is a fascinating site.

A fuzzy photo of a fuzzy creature

Just Plain Weird

We'll say one thing for the writers at **The Fortean Times Online** (http://www.forteantimes.com/): they know how to craft a good opening sentence. Exhibit A: "Last year, there was widespread fear in Zanzibar concerning the return of the popobawa, a dwarf with a Cyclops eye, small pointed ears, bat wings and talons, notorious for swooping into houses and raping men." They're pretty good with article titles, too; that one is entitled "Bat-Winged Sex Dwarf." Ghosts, UFOs, ESP, goatsuckers, Bigfoot, rains of frogs, holy messages in eggplants, spontaneous human combustion, time travel, and a whole brew of conspiracies and unexplained phenomena are the stuff of this eccentric magazine.

Here are some typical news items:

- In a remote field in Victoria, Australia, the body of a man is found; he is dressed in a tight-fitting fish suit.
- A man bursts into a New Zealand radio station, takes the manager hostage, and demands that the station play "Rainbow Connection" by Kermit the Frog.
- A shower of frogs rains down upon some tourists in Scotland. (The article does not state whether they were singing "Rainbow Connection.")

We were tempted to scoff at some of the Fortean Times' stories until we saw the photographic evidence in an article that sets out to prove the moon landings were faked. Hey! Shadows are cast in different directions, indicating multiple light sources, which implies a movie set. Boy, NASA had better have a good explanation for this!

Astronauts on the moon? We think not.
© John Brown Publishing/Fortean Times

Help! Call the CSICOPs!

If, after a careful perusal of this chapter, you feel a stronger kinship for The Amazing Randi than Those Amazing Aliens, perhaps you should subscribe to **The Skeptical Inquirer** (http://www.csicop.org/si). As you can imagine, this magazine is "a devastating exercise in debunking," as the *Washington Post* put it. With a head-shaking sort of bemusement and an arsenal of scientific studies, its writers cluck sarcastically at believers in UFOs, Bigfoot, ghosts, ESP, psychics, touch healing, astrology, aliens, "The X-Files," and every other kind of paranormal, pseudoscientific phenomenon.

To be honest, we worship this publication. We adore its publisher (the Committee for the Scientific Investigation of Claims of the Paranormal, or CSICOP). Everything they print is absolutely true . . . absolutely sensible . . . and absolutely indisputable. There *is* nothing paranormal. There *are* no government coverups. There *are* no space aliens.

The voices from our brain implants told us so.

Greetings From
The Weird Wide Web

All Creatures Great and Not So Great

Would you like some tips on keeping cockroaches as pets? No? Well, how about 24-hour-a-day access to a colony of naked mole-rats? Not interested? Hmm. Perhaps you'd like to know what kind of tricks you can teach a Sea Monkey? Not in this lifetime, eh? Want to look at some photos of really cute hamsters? You'd rather cut off your own head with a shovel?

Well, gosh, maybe you'd better just skip to the next chapter then.

Our Six-Legged Pals

It has 18 knees and a skeleton on the outside of its body. It's hard to kill: it can live up to a month without food; it can survive in temperatures as low as 32 degrees Fahrenheit; its body contains a white, fatty substance that absorbs and neutralizes poisons; it will live for a week even if you chop off its head! A monster from a low-budget horror movie? Nope. We're talking about a creature that is probably living under your refrigerator right now: the cockroach. If you're hankering to learn more about cockroaches, there's no better place than **Cockroach World** (http://www.nj.com/yucky/roaches/index.html).

This is no boring entomological site: Cockroach World is a multimedia extravaganza that includes sound files of hissing roaches, movies of roaches that spit on you and emit a foul odor, and photos of some of the 5,000 roach species found worldwide. If you're enamored of the little fellows, you'll enjoy the instructive section on catching roaches and keeping them as pets. If you're normal, you'll enjoy the section on killing them with boric acid.

Your hostess, entomologist Dr. Betty Faber (aka "The Bug Lady") narrates the audio and video clips and answers the Web-surfing public's roach-related questions. When we looked in, the question of the week was: "Can I get rid of cockroaches using natural predators?" Betty replies that "centipedes, spiders, scorpions, lizards, tarantulas, rats, and mice all like to eat cockroaches."

We can only surmise that next week's question will be: "How do I get rid of all the centipedes, spiders, scorpions, lizards, tarantulas, rats, and mice in my house?"

Betty the Bug Lady and her friends

Betty doesn't have a monopoly on roaches. Here we will exhibit a modicum of sophistication, not only by using the word "modicum" but by refraining from saying the Web is crawling with roach sites. Even though it is.

If you visit **Joe's Apartment** (http://www.joesapt.com) you'll encounter some roach facts (although not nearly as many as Betty offers) and glimpses into roach culture, including a karaoke-style sing-along featuring songs such as "Funky Towel." Click on Joe's computer and you'll be able to access roachified parodies of popular online services and 'zines.

If you're looking for a more highbrow cockroach site, visit the **Blattodea Culture Group** (http://www.ex.ac.uk/~gjlramel/bcg.html). This British organization "aims to promote the study and culture of cockroaches on a world wide basis . . . as well as maintaining a policy of free distribution of excess livestock between members." (I say, old chap, could you spare a Madagascar Hissing Cockroach or two?)

The members are obviously quite fond of their little cockroach pals, as evidenced by the following photo, entitled "Lopsided Wally." Anybody who names a roach Lopsided Wally is OK in our book. (And this *is* our book, after all.)

Lopsided Wally the Cockroach

Like Betty the Bug Lady and Joe, the Blattodea Culture Group thinks roaches are just the bee's knees. And they advocate keeping them as pets (the roaches, not Betty and Joe). Detailed care-and-feeding instructions are provided—although we think we might draw the line at providing our roaches with a heating pad as they suggest. Heating pads, the instructions point out, come in a variety of shapes and sizes, "and it is best to talk to your local seller as to what you need." This should make for some amusing discussions with hardware store employees.

Finally, for a look at cockroaches in the arts, the libretto for **"Lament Del Cockroach,"** a mini-operetta for Nobel Laureates and mezzo-sopranos, can be found at http://www.eecs.harvard.edu/ig_nobel/libretto.html.

For another perspective on insects, try neuroscientist Andrew Giger's **B-EYE** page (http://cvs.anu.edu.au/andy/beye/beyehome.html), which lets you see the world through the eyes of a honeybee.

Why would you want to see like a bee? That is the question.

Yes, We Have No Banana Slugs (Thanks to George Deukmejian)

If gastropods are your cup of tea (not literally, we hope), you'll like the **Slugs** page at http://www.teleport.com/~jleon/slugs.html. It offers numerous photographs of slugs in their natural habitat, including a banana slug, which is the official mascot of the University of California, Santa Cruz. At UCSC's **Banana Slug Home Page** (http://www.slugs.com/slugweb/slug_home_page.html) you learn some fascinating facts about banana slugs, such as (a) they're hermaphrodites; (b) they can grow to 10 inches in length; and (c) they almost became the Official State Mollusk of California—a bill to that effect passed the State Senate and Assembly in 1988 but was, alas, vetoed by Governor George Deukmejian.

For the quintessential list of **Slug Links,** see http://home.earthlink.net/~lejones/sluglink.htm. Here you'll find many pages devoted to slugs, although some of the references point to band names and other non-gastropodal subjects.

Unlike cockroaches, nobody seems to be interested in keeping slugs as pets. Go figure.

Sea Monkeys!

Comic books used to be a great way to introduce kids to life's major disappointments. From ads on the back page you could order all sorts of products that didn't live up to their billing. X-Ray Specs didn't really let you see through women's clothing. The Charles Atlas fitness program transformed you from a 90-pound weakling into a 100-pound weakling. And, perhaps worst of all, Sea Monkeys weren't really cute little aquatic monkeys with smiling faces, as shown in the pictures: they were just brine shrimp.

Well, these days the Web has replaced comic books when it comes to disappointing little children. There you'll find several sites devoted to Sea Monkeys, including **The Sea Monkey Worship Page** (http://users.uniserve.com/ ~sbarclay/seamonk.htm).

Idealized Sea Monkeys

Like the comic-book ads of yore, this page can get you pretty fired up about Sea Monkeys. Here, for example, is an excerpt from the *Official Sea Monkey Handbook*: "You are about to begin a NEW amazing hobby that is so fantastic, it STAGGERS THE IMAGINATION! . . . As a creator of Sea-Monkeys®, you share with [fellow hobbyists] the knowledge that through your willingness to explore the unknown, you have stepped across the threshold of one of the strange worlds of tomorrow's science . . . TODAY!" Wow! (You know, if the person who wrote this copy were to be hired by banana-slug aficionados, perhaps slugs—renamed Forest Loam Monkeys—would be more popular as pets.)

The Sea Monkey Worship Page is an eclectic blend of scientific information and Sea Monkey boosterism. Here you'll learn that Sea Monkeys (*Artemis nyos*) have three eyes, breathe through their feet, and can reproduce sexually or asexually. You can also read poems about Sea Monkeys (death is a popular theme) and learn a bit about Sea Monkey creator Mr. Harold von Braunhut. (Not content to rest on his laurels, Mr. von Braunhut has a new project up his sleeve: tiny pet lobsters!) You'll also learn how to teach tricks to your Sea Monkeys. Turns out they're pretty much one-trick monkeys; the "trick" is getting them to follow a beam of light. One enterprising owner suggested putting a batch of Sea Monkeys in a drink, dimming the lights, then moving a flashlight in a circular pattern over the top of the glass, causing the Sea Monkeys to stir the drink.

Who says you can't find useful information on the Web?

Rodents: The Good, the Bald, and the Ugly

You can learn a lot about hamsters on the Web. For starters, we learned that *hamstery* is a noun. (We always thought it was an adjective, as in "Rayette, have you aired out the kids' room lately? It smells kind of hamstery in there.") It turns out that a hamstery is an outfit that breeds hamsters.

The premier hamstery site is the **Northbow Hamstery** (http://www.cnw.com/~ibis/northbow). The opening statement says, "We think you will enjoy this site even if you are not a hamster breeder." We think so, too. For example, if you're a sadist, you'll enjoy "Hamster Noises: Digitized sounds from an upset baby hamster." If you're a masochist, you'll enjoy the strains of peppy music that play continuously as animated hamsters frolic across the opening screen. And almost everyone will enjoy the section entitled "Neutered Hamsters: All about hamster neutering and why."

The site includes links to other noteworthy hamster sites, including that of Britain's **National Hamster Council** (http://www.acmepet.com/non-profit/nhc.html) and a Japanese page that includes a movie called **The Great Escape Movie Hamster** (http://www.bekkoame.or.jp/~yakkun/escape.html). The movie's no **Godzilla** (http://www.ultranet.com/~barry/godmain.htm), but it's a gripping tale nonetheless.

The sun never sets on the hamsters.

Alas, it's not a talkie, but here are a few excerpts from the text synopsis: "One day, he escaped from the cage. He thought, 'yah, I'm free. I can go elsewhere, nobody can stop me.' Then, he enjoyed freedom. But his freedom did not keep long. . . . The evil hand catched him." You'll laugh. You'll cry. You'll wonder why you're spending good money on an Internet connection.

Here is a photo of Beethoven (1995-1996), one of the many hamsters at the Northbow Hamstery. (No, he's not on fire; he's just having a bad fur day.)

The hamster: A cute, furry rodent

Beethoven, despite his unruly fur, is arguably a cute animal. The animal pictured next is arguably the least cute animal on the planet — sort of the Antihamster.

The naked mole-rat: A hideous, hairless rodent

Naked mole-rats are fascinating African rodents. Thanks to the National Zoo's **Naked Mole-Rat Colony Cam** (http://www.si.edu/organiza/museums/zoo/hilights/webcams/molerat1/nmcamtl.htm), you can watch these creatures in action any time, day or night. Well, maybe "action" is stretching it a bit — naked mole-rats spend most of their time lying around in a pile.

At first you might think you've accidentally accessed the wrong Web site and are looking at a plate of Vienna sausages (see http://www.orci.com/personal/jim/vienna.html for a collection of **Vienna Sausage Labels**). But if you view the time-lapse sequence, which features a new shot every three minutes, you'll realize that naked mole-rats are actually slightly more animated than your average Vienna sausages (although somewhat less cute).

Here are some highlights from the Naked Mole-Rat Cam:

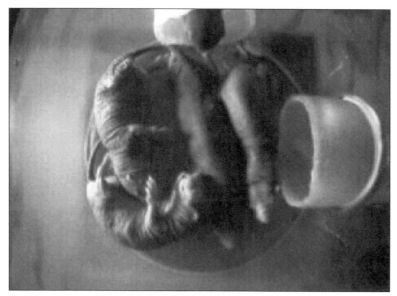

Naked mole-rats lying around

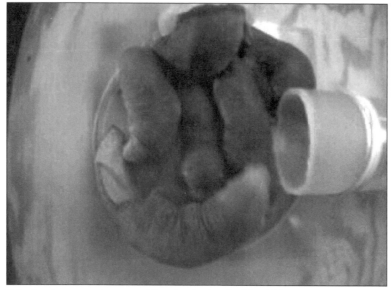

Naked mole-rats eating something that looks a lot like SPAM

In the unlikely event that you want to find out more about naked mole-rats, we'd suggest Portland's **Metro Washington Park Zoo** page (http://engine.caboose.com/a1topics/portland_zoo/maingate/africa/Naked_Mole_Rat), where you learn that naked mole-rats (aka Sand Puppies, which is a *much* cuter name) have wrinkled, flesh-toned skin, sparse hair, tiny eyes, a dearth of sweat glands, and abundant body oils. With that in mind, it should come as no surprise that their social lives are a bit lackluster. Mole-rats are *eusocial* animals, which means they live in colonies led by a single dominant female called a queen, much like ants, bees, or England. They spend most of their time underground, digging burrows, grubbing for tubers, and hoping for their big break posing for a naked mole-rat cam.

Remote Cats

Michael Witbrock, who lives in Pittsburgh, owns a cat. If you do not know Michael Witbrock and live nowhere near Pittsburgh—which applies to most of the people reading this book—but still have a yearning to talk to Michael's cat, you're in luck. Michael has set up a voice synthesizer on his home computer that will speak any words that you type at his **Talk to My Cat** site (http://queer.slip.cs.cmu.edu/cgi-bin/talktocat?). The cat, which likes to sit near the computer, will hear your words wafting from the computer's speaker and do what cats always do: ignore them.

A lengthy transcript of things people have said to the cat is available at the site. Of the more than 75,000 people who have talked to the cat so far, we'd estimate that around 73,000 of them said something along the lines of "Here, kitty, kitty" or "Woof." This does not say much for the intelligence and creativity of the international community of World Wide Web users. If you think you might be tempted to say something inane such as "Here, kitty, kitty" to Michael's cat, we urge you to check out *Talking to Cats on the Web For Dummies* from IDG Books. [Editor's note: They're kidding. That book won't be out for another year.] If you don't yet have a Web connection (or a life), you also have the option of sending e-mail to the cat.

If you're not the talkative type, you can always **Wave to the Cats** at http://hogwild.hamjudo.com/cgi-bin/wave. At this site you click a button that activates a robotic hand that waves to Paul Haas's cats (if they're in the room). A list of options lets you control how fervently the hand waves. Not that this makes much difference to the cats, of course. According to Mr. Haas's observations, three of his four cats ignore the hand. The other one stares at the hand, which is pretty much beyond the call of duty for a cat. Maybe someday someone will set up a remotely activated device that opens a can of tuna—then we'd see some results! (Alternatively, someone could set up a site that waves to dogs, who might actually give a damn.)

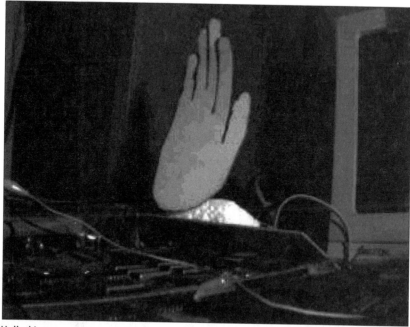

Hello, kitty

Not with a Bang...

After you've waved a final goodbye to your pet, you might find some solace at the **Rainbow Bridge Tribute** page (http://www.primenet.com/~meggie/bridge.htm) or the **Virtual Pet Cemetery** (http://www.lavamind.com/pet.html). Here you'll find tributes to many feathered and furry friends (no cockroaches—yet) who have passed on. Having lost a few furry friends ourselves, we're not going to make fun of these sites (although the account of Maurice the hamster's suicide pushed us dangerously close to snickering). In fact, they're actually kind of touching.

If your pet dies suddenly and unexpectedly (a suicide, for example), you may not be emotionally prepared to part with the little guy's remains. That's where pet mummification comes in. For $14,000, you can have your pet's body mummified and placed in a custom bronze mummiform case by **Summum Mummification** (http://www.summum.org/mum.htm). Summum's technicians use modern chemistry to keep your pet's body fresh and supple for a long time. How long? "Ron Temu, a licensed embalmer and a future mummy himself, is convinced they will be good for thousands of years."

Like Ron Temu, you can opt to have yourself mummified in addition to your pet. So far, Summum founder Corky Ra and his team have mummified dogs, cats, and birds; they have yet to mummify a person (except for practice). But you could be the first. Think of it this way: Summum's procedure can preserve the genetic codes within the cells so well that someday in the future, when cloning is perfected, you and your beloved hamster could be reunited. It's worth a try.

Goodbye, kitty

And speaking of dead animals (masterful segues such as that are the hallmark of us professional writers), this chapter would not be complete without a reference to the **Exploding Whale** page (http://alt.xmission.com:80/ ~grue/whale/). This site includes digital video of a TV newscaster reporting a grisly incident involving an eight-ton dead whale, a half ton of dynamite, and the Oregon State Highway Division.

The newscaster

Oregon, it seems, does not have a Dead Behemoth Removal Division, so the Highway Division was called in to dispose of a rather ripe whale that had washed up on the beach near the town of Florence.

The whale

The plan—which sounded pretty good in theory—was to blow the whale into thousands of little blubber bits, which would then be consumed by seagulls, crabs, and other creatures unconcerned about their daily fat intake. Well, it started off well enough, with a colossal explosion and riotous cheers from the spectators.

Ka-boom! Blubber bits

The spectators changed their tune, however, when whale chunks large enough to flatten a Buick (which one did) began raining down in their midst. Fortunately, nobody was hurt, but everyone within a quarter mile of the blast was spattered with rotting whale gore. Most were not amused.

The seagulls fled the scene, which left a handful of sheepish highway workers to bury the substantial hunks of whale carcass that remained on the beach.

The aftermath

This unfortunate incident has taught us much about the ratio of dynamite to blubber necessary for successful whale detonation. However, if any novice whale recyclers are operating in the neighborhood, we think we'll just watch it on TV, thanks.

Greetings from
The Weird Wide Web

Weird Science

The average person, when crushing a soda can, generally crimps the can in the middle to make it collapse more easily, places it on the ground, and stomps it flat. A scientist, on the other hand, is likely to use high-temperature, magnetically confined plasma, placing the can in a copper coil inside a device with a 47 µF, 10 kV capacitor switched with a spark-gap, then charging up the capacitor, which discharges through the coil, concentrating the plasma and producing a magnetic field so strong that it crushes the can. (See the **Can Crusher Homepage** at http://hibp.ecse.rpi.edu/~chowm/can_crusher.html for more info.)

Similarly, a regular Joe or Jane, if asked how to move a piano, might give a pathetically unimaginative reply such as, "Call a piano mover?" An innovator, however—the kind of visionary we're talking about in this chapter—would reconstruct a gigantic mediaeval siege engine and catapult the piano sky-high. That's the difference between scientists and the rest of us: they think big. Some might say, too big—as in the case of the Aludium Q-36 Pumpkin Modulator described later in this chapter—but who are we to judge?

We begin with a brief look at some bizarre inventions of yore.

Michael Colitz is a patent attorney with a patently ingenious idea: attract potential clients to his Web site by featuring, each month, another of the world's most **Wacky Patents** (http://www.colitz.com/site/wacky.htm). Drawn from the actual archives of the U.S. Patent Office of days gone by (the late 1800s seemed to be the wackiest period, patentwise), these carefully illustrated, crisply described contraptions probably never won their inventors a nickel—although being immortalized on the Internet 100 years later is nothing to sneeze at.

Who knew that Big Bird was actually patented in 1888?

You'll find, for example, the Audible Tooth Brush ("to cleanse the teeth and in doing so cause musical sounds to interest and entertain the user"); the Washing Machine Having Means for Attaching Same to a Vehicle Wheel (neatly solving the age-old dilemma: go for a Sunday drive or do the laundry?); the Nylon Hose Treated With Microencapsulated Hair Dissolving Solution (imagine the hapless bank robber who uses one of these as a disguise!); the indispensable Combined Grocer's Package, Grater, Slicer and Mouse and Fly Trap (cheese grater *and* fly trap? Honey, I think I'll have my pasta without the parmesan tonight); and the frightening Apparatus for Facilitating the Birth of a Child by Centrifugal Force—essentially a woman-sized turntable and a pair of netted underpants to prevent the baby from being smashed against the hospital-room walls.

(We're pretty sure Evel Knievel's mom used one of these. To learn all about **Evel Knievel,** who is now a celebrity spokesman for pain relievers and bike helmets [how the mighty have fallen, as it were], you can visit his site at http://www.evelknievel.com/.)

The era of wacky inventions by no means ended in the 1800s. Mad scientists are alive and well on the World Wide Web. From Rube Goldberg inventions (a liquid nitrogen-powered bottle-rocket) to bizarre scientific experiments (are leeches more likely to suck blood from a human arm if it is slathered with sour cream?), you'll find them somewhere in cyberspace.

Mad Scientists on Parade

The contemporary crop of mad scientists, evil geniuses, and loony inventors has carved out its own little corner of the Web. Their scientific efforts can be divided into three major categories: 1) shooting things real far, 2) blowing things up, or 3) both.

We reiterate the warnings posted on most of these pages and caution you never, never, never to try these experiments at home. Or in the church basement. Or anywhere, for that matter. The experiments described here were performed by highly trained technical experts and/or guys who were willing to sacrifice an eye or two in the name of science.

For example, some of the boys at the Advanced Graphics Division (AGD) of Silicon Graphics, Inc. (SGI) enjoy conducting the occasional diabolical science experiment (DSE) in their spare time. Dominic Giampaolo, a former SGI employee, put together a page—the **AGD Antics and Mayhem Page** (http://www.be.com/~dbg/antics/index.html)—that shows some of their shenanigans . . . er, that is, *research.*

When our heroes saw an ad for a 3-foot by $2^1/_2$-foot Fresnel lens, they had to have it. According to the ad, the lens could heat surfaces up to 3,000 degrees Fahrenheit and melt asphalt in seconds. They decided to test their new weapon on the most indestructible substance known to Man: SPAM. No problem; the thing immolated a tin of SPAM in no time. The SPAM had the last laugh, however, as evidenced by this researcher's notes: "Interestingly, that can of SPAM has sat, open, in my office for over 3 months now. It has not shown one sign of mold or decay. Think about that." We don't want to!

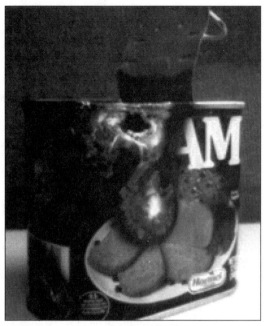

SPAM finally meets its match.

One of the SGI gang, Mark Leather, has his own science-experiment page, which features the **Alhambra Water Bottle Rocket** (http://reality.sgi.com/employees/mark/alrocket/). In his site, he chronicles his attempts to launch a five-gallon plastic water bottle into low earth orbit, using liquid nitrogen as a fuel.

One of your present authors is acquainted with Mr. Leather, who is a quiet, unassuming man until you get him talking about science experiments. At a recent dinner party, he was seen pensively fingering a grape during dessert, then was heard shyly asking the hostess, "You don't by any chance have any liquid nitrogen, do you?" His disappointment was palpable when she responded in the negative. (Hostess tip: always keep plenty of liquefied gases on hand when inviting scientists to a dinner party!) He was in a somewhat better humor a few weeks later, when we invited him over to help stick electrodes into a dill pickle and light it up (see Chapter 1, "Fun with Food").

Mad-scientist aficionados will also enjoy the **Rocket Trike** page (http://132.241.70.202/sps/activities/rocket_trike.html). In the name of automotive research, a group of nutty Cal State scientists duct-taped a fire extinguisher to the back of an oversized tricycle. [Lawyer's note: DON'T DO IT.] We doubt this is the sort of vehicle you'll see slowly turning on a gleaming turntable at your local auto show. Nor do we imagine that a fire extinguisher provides much in the way of thrust. Even so, what cop could resist asking the Rocket Trike rider: "Hey, pal, where's the fire?"

Our favorite invention is Steve Mann's **Smart underwear** (http://n1nlf-1.
media.mit.edu/smart_clothing/node4.html#SECTION00022000000000000000).
Mann, a graduate student at MIT, has come up with a concept he calls
"smart clothing." His inventions focus on a cyborgian interaction between
human and machine, where a mechanical device can extend a person's
capabilities without requiring any conscious effort. Smart underwear (not
yet available at Kmart, since it's in the prototype stage) allows the wearer
to effortlessly control the temperature in a room.

Here's how it works. The underwear has a sweat-detection sensor sewn
into the waistband. A transmitter antenna sends signals to a receiver and
bank of relays which control a heater. When the wearer begins to sweat,
the apparatus turns down the heat; when the sweat level decreases, it
cranks up the heat. This seamless melding of man and machine (and underwear) is no doubt the wave of the future. Remember, you read it here first.

Unexplained phenomena? Unconventional inventions or theories?
They've got 'em at the **Weird Research, Anomalous Physics** page (http://
www.eskimo.com/~billb/weird.html). Ball lightning, the Taos Hum, antigrav-
ity devices, **Tesla Coils** (see also http://www.ocws.com/tesla/index.html), cold
fusion . . . it's all here. This site is a clearinghouse for mad scientists, offering information on organizations, literature, and discussion groups, as
well as plenty of links to other mad-scientist sites. The "For Sale" section
is particularly engrossing. Some examples:

- ✳ Laser rod, ruby (pink synthetic corundum)
- ✳ Four-inch spark (output approx. 75 KV AC, 60 Hz) high voltage
  supply kit . . . For those experienced with HV only!
- ✳ Own a Piece of the Bomb—Sand fused by atomic tests in
  White Sands, NM
- ✳ Giant pulse-discharge capacitors
- ✳ XRay screens—plastic screens with rare earth lanthanum
  oxybromide phosphor fluoresce blue when exposed to xrays
- ✳ Levitation Device prototype—"the patent covers stabilizing
  forces associated with the magnetic levitation of various mag-
  netic embodiments through induced eddy currents in a con-
  ductor . . . A prototype has been sold to the US Air Force and
  Mattel Toy company has expressed interest in the technology
  as well." [Our take: If the U.S. Military *and* Mattel are interested in a technology, it's probably a winner. "Deploy the
  Levitating Barbies™, men! We're goin' in!" Blam! Blam!
  "Aaaaaaagh!"]

High-voltage hijinx with a Tesla coil

Speaking of scientists gone awry, an organization actually exists that bestows awards on the maddest scientists they can find. It's the **Ig Nobel Prizes,** given each year by an outfit called the Annals of Improbable Research (http://www.eecs.harvard.edu/ig_nobel/). The lucky recipients are scientists whose experiments "cannot, and should not, be reproduced."

For example, in *The European Journal of Physics*, Robert Matthews published a paper called "Tumbling Toast, Murphy's Law and the Fundamental Constants." In this study, he attempts to prove or disprove the theorem that a piece of toast knocked off the breakfast table inevitably lands butter side down. Surprise, surprise: "It turns out that the public perception is quite correct. Toast does indeed have a natural tendency to land butter side down, essentially because the gravitation torque induced as the toast topples over the edge of the plate/table is insufficient to bring the toast butter-side up again by the time it hits the floor." Who knew?

The Web site notes that some of the prizes' recipients failed to appear to receive their trophies. By sheerest coincidence, the absentees largely fall into the category of People Awarded the Ig Nobel Prize Sarcastically, such as the R.J. Reynolds Tobacco company scientist who testified to Congress that nicotine is not addictive, or France's President, who "commemorated the fiftieth anniversary of Hiroshima with atomic bomb tests in the Pacific."

But a few of the studies will live on as truly inspired tugs on the scientific envelope. Take the experiment called "Effect of Ale, Garlic, and Soured Cream on the Appetite of Leeches." These well-meaning Norwegian scientists intended to study whether garlic, as legend would have it, actually acts as a vampire repellent. Unfortunately, no vampires volunteered for the experiment, so the Norwegians substituted the closest bloodsuckers they could persuade to participate—leeches.

As it happens, leeches were actually *attracted*, not repelled, by garlic-soaked human flesh. While they were at it, the scientists also immersed the leeches in two other substances with legendary properties: beer and sour cream. The sour cream produced no change in leeches' likelihood of sucking one's blood. As for the beer, however: "After having been exposed to beer, some of the leeches changed behaviour, swaying their forebodies, losing grip or falling on their backs."

Not to mention the scientists.

Look! Up in the Sky! It's a . . . Buick!

Picture the following pastoral scene: a flock of sheep grazes placidly amid the rolling hills of the English countryside; tendrils of mist rise from the verdant meadow; the liquid notes of a lark waft from a nearby hedgerow; a 500-pound dead pig parachutes down.

Ah, yes, you'd be at Hew Kennedy's place then. Mr. Kennedy has built a working siege engine, also called a *trebuchet* (pronounced TRAY-boo-shay) and enjoys nothing better than lobbing heavy objects—pianos, cars, and deceased livestock—across the grounds of his 620-acre estate.

Although Mr. Kennedy's trebuchet is used for purely recreational purposes (mostly because hog-lobbing has few commercial applications), in the 1300s these machines were early instruments of germ warfare, employed to hurl diseased animal carcasses over the walls of besieged castles. (They were also, as one trebuchet site points out, an early form of shuttle diplomacy, occasionally sending an unsuccessful ambassador back where he came from.)

The trebuchet consists of a giant beam, weighted at one end, that pivots on an axle. On the non-weighted end is a steel-cable sling. A projectile is attached to the sling, and the weighted end is raised into the air and then dropped, flinging the missile across the countryside. While **Hew Kennedy** (http://asylum.apocalypse.org/pub/u/zonker/fpp/html/trebuchet.html) is the acknowledged king of modern trebuchet builders, many young whippersnappers (and a few middle-aged whippersnappers) are following in his illustrious footsteps. Quite a trebuchet revival is taking place, as you'll see if you visit Andrew Ryan's **Trebuchets are Back** site at http://www.contrib.andrew.cmu.edu/~ar39/trebuchets.html. Here you'll find diagrams of the device, photos of a flying piano, a photo of Andrew's dad standing next to a trebuchet, and links to other trebuchet resources, including an article on **Richard Clifford and John Quincy** (http://outside.starwave.com:80/magazine/0895/8f_bird.html), who plan to build the world's largest trebuchet. (They're Texans.)

Tourist and trebuchet

If you follow some of these links, you'll discover that, in addition to the ever-popular piano, *objets du trebuchet* include bowling balls, cars, dead horses (favored by traditionalists), cases of SPAM, toilets, sinks, and **Ron Toms and his friends** (http://www.rlt.com/pub/trebuchet/). It seems that Mr. Toms, in a moment of *joie de vivre* (pronounced stoo-PID-i-tee), decided to use his homemade trebuchet to fling himself into the air. One might be tempted to question Mr. Toms' sanity; unlike the aforementioned dead pig, he wasn't even wearing a parachute.

Before launching himself, however, Mr. Toms took the precaution of (a) consulting experts, and (b) testing the device. No matter that the experts—a physics professor and a mechanical engineering professor—told him the acceleration would probably rip his head off. And so what if the test load—a 55-gallon drum partially filled with water—flew straight up and fell straight down, crushing the trebuchet? He rebuilt the contraption, performed a few more tests, went down to the local river with his friends, climbed on, and fired away. After he survived his 30-foot-high arc into the river, his friends tried it too. Oddly enough, no one was injured or killed, even when the device eventually snapped apart in mid-fling. This is the kind of pioneering spirit that makes America great—and keeps our population growth in check.

Cutting-Edge Veggie-Chuckin' Technology

Now, you could certainly use a trebuchet to lob pumpkins at the annual Pumpkin Chuckin' contest in Lewes, Delaware. Many do. But these days you'd be outgunned. You'd find yourself up against some serious pumpkin-firing hardware such as air cannons, which are gigantic air tanks pressurized by industrial jackhammer compressors, sporting barrels 20 feet long or more. These babies can whip a pumpkin more than 2,000 feet quicker than you can say "Aaaagh! Look out for that pum—". (If the distance records keep improving at the current rate, they're going to have to hold the contest in a larger state.) Some of the cannons from the 1996 competition are described at Discovery Channel Online's **alt.tech.pumpkin** site at http://eagle.online.discovery.com/DCO/doc/1012/world/alttech/alttech 112396/alttech.html. [Authors' note: You're just going to have to take our word that this site exists; there's no way you're going to type all that without making a mistake.]

The people who build these air cannons aren't kidding around. For example, a team of commandos from Morton, Illinois, rolled into the 1996 Pumpkin Chuckin' competition with an olive-drab behemoth sporting a barrel more than 50 feet long. They had vertical and horizontal barrel motion capability, they had muzzle velocity sensors, they had an on-board computer. The payload was propelled by a tank filled with pressurized air at 600 psi. This was the Mother of All Pumpkin Chuckers, the **Aludium Q-36 Pumpkin Modulator,** which is reverently chronicled at http://www.voicenet.com/~surge42/q36.htm. An onlooker describes the pre-chuck preparation: "Each time they filled the main gun tank the pressurized air would hiss. As the pressurized air passed into the larger tank it started vibrating. A low but very audible sonic hum oozed out, you could feel it in your chest. It appeared the whole gun was resonating. The sound was supernatural. It was the sound of PURE MECHANICAL POWER!"

The Q-36 shot a pumpkin 2,710 feet, handily winning the distance contest. It was also the first device to blow a hole completely through a wooden target. In the wrong hands, this thing could be a formidable weapon. We sincerely hope the Aludium Q-36 Pumpkin Modulator doesn't fall into the clutches of a militant yokel group with a large stockpile of pumpkins. (We also hope Ron Toms doesn't get hold of it.)

"P" minus 20 and counting: The Aludium Q-36 Pumpkin Modulator stands by.

Fortunately, you don't have to build a giant catapult to enjoy the fun of flinging vegetables through the air. You can do so in the privacy of your own home, as you'll discover on the **Backyard Ballistics** page (http://www2. csn.net/~bsimon/backyard.html). Here you'll find instructions for building your own Spud Gun. (The author assures us that this device is *not* considered a firearm by the Bureau of Alcohol, Tobacco, and Firearms.) It's a dandy little spudzooka capable of flinging raw or half-baked potatoes up to 220 yards. What better way to spend a lazy summer afternoon than to fill your neighbors' lawns with potato salad?

Of course, building home weapons systems is not without risk. This Web page bears the legend, "WARNING: These things have a tendency to attract every 8-12 year old kid in the neighborhood."

They're Not All Geeks

Do you think of scientists as nerdy, scrawny, pocket protector-wearing geeks with thick glasses, rumpled clothing, and unkempt hair? Well, yeah, we do too. But not all scientists fit this stereotype—and we have the pin-up pix to prove it. **The Studmuffins of Science** calendar (http://www.studmuffins.com/index.html) is the brainchild of Karen Hopkin, who decided that the world needed a beefcake calendar that showed off twelve brawny brains. The requirements: a Ph.D. and a Y chromosome. Being a hunk didn't hurt.

Although the idea started out as a joke, Dr. Hopkin (who has a Ph.D. in biochemistry herself) received so many requests for the calendar that she decided she'd better create one. So she posted an ad on a science-oriented electronic bulletin board, and the nominations came pouring in. She reviewed photos, conducted interviews, and selected twelve hunks to pose for the calendar. "Designed to show PhDs at work and at play, the calendar features a dozen handsome, fun-loving, accomplished scientists, swimming, biking, skating, and enjoying some time away from the lab."

Bennett Link, 1997's "Dr. April"

You can take a peek at the 1996 and 1997 studmuffins at the site, and order the calendar if you like what you see ("Oooh! Look, Shirley—a Nobel Laureate! Just look at the accolades on that guy!"). These fellows are far from nerdy-looking; not one of them is wearing a pocket protector —of course, they're not wearing pockets, either. You also learn a bit about each guy—his likes and dislikes, and perhaps his favorite theorem and his current research topic. But let's face it, gals—you're more interested in their abs than their labs.

Greetings from The Weird Wide Web

The Final Chapter

If you're reading this, chances are pretty good that you're not dead. We hate to be the ones to bring this up, but sooner or later you will die, dear reader. As a public service, this chapter directs you to numerous Web sites that will help you come to terms with that fact. Actually, most of the sites described here will help you come to terms with the fact that lots of *other* people are dead—but perhaps you can extrapolate from that and ponder your own mortality.

Now, if you dwell on such sites for too long, your ponderings may well lead you to a deep, philosophical insight such as "Yippee! All these people are dead and I'm not!" That's not quite what we had in mind, but we suppose it will do. [Author's note: At least that sentiment is, as we say in California, "life-affirming."] [Other author's note: Or, as we say in New York, "a crock."]

Dead Celebrities

One evening, you're sitting there watching reruns of *Green Acres* and you think to yourself, "You know, you sure don't hear much about Eddie Albert these days. I wonder if he's still alive. And what about Eva Gabor?" (It's a pretty safe bet that Arnold the Pig has snuffled off this mortal coil by now.)

Well, if you can drag yourself from one tube to another and fire up the Web, you can find out if these two—and a host of other celebrities—are still kicking. You'll find a comprehensive list of dead celebrities—and numerous live ones that you may be wondering about—at the **Dead People Server** (http://www.scarletfire.com/dps/), an invaluable resource put together by Jim Petersen. For those celebrities who have faded to black, the Dead People Server lists the date and cause of death. (For example, "Curt Cobain (musician)—Dead. Angst. Apr 8, 1994.")

And then there's Jim Tipton, who likes to dish celebrity dirt. No, not gossip; we mean he collects *actual* dirt, from the gravesites of noteworthy people. Frankly, we frown on collecting dirt from gravesites. If everyone did that, all the noteworthy people would be unearthed in no time, leaving gaping holes in cemeteries across the world and making Forest Lawn look like a piece of Swiss cheese. But if you enjoy visiting graves, Tipton's **Find-A-Grave** site (http://www.orci.com/personal/jim/index.html) can come in handy. Here, you'll find the gravesite locations of more than a thousand people.

Keep in mind that not everyone on Tipton's list is a celebrity; they're simply noteworthy. Some are more noteworthy than others. For example, the first name in the alphabetical listing is Cleveland Abbe. Well, sure, you're saying, he was the first weather forecaster—everybody knows that! And how about Bernt Balchen (Admiral Perry's pilot) and Elmer Berger (inventor of the rear-view mirror)? Well, OK, in hindsight, maybe Elmer Berger should be considered noteworthy.

A similar site is the **Tombstone Tourist** (http://www.teleport.com/~stanton), where Scott Stanton, a veteran of 2,000 grave visits, each month profiles a dead pop singer and his grave. Sample writeup: "Andy Gibb's ferocious cocaine habit was causing him serious problems by the early 1980s. In 1985, Andy was admitted to the Betty Ford Clinic. Unfortunately, the damage had been done and just five days after his 30th birthday, Andy Gibb died. His body was flown back to the U.S. to his final resting place at Forest Lawn, Hollywood Hills. From Freeway 134, take the Forest Lawn Drive exit in the city of Burbank. Follow the signs to the cemetery to the gated entrance. Andy is located on the outside wall which faces the entrance to the cemetery closest to Ascension Road."

A fitting epitaph
Photo: Dave Champagne, DC Studios

Actually, the Tombstone Tourist page's most noteworthy aspect is that Kathie Lee Gifford called it "the most disgusting page on the Internet." Kathie Lee needs to get out more (or should we say, "stay in more"?). If she thinks the Tombstone Tourist is disgusting, then what's the decomposing lunchmeat at the Spam Cam site — chopped liver?

Thanks to the labors of friends and fans, some dead celebrities have their own pages. Timothy Leary is dead, but his memory lives on at the **Timothy Leary** page at http://www.leary.com:8081/intro/index.html or, alternatively, http://www.interverse.com/~leary/index.html. At this extensive site, you can read about Dr. Leary's checkered (make that paisleyed) career, chat with like-minded pilgrims, or take a virtual tour of his Los Angeles house, guided by a digital simulacrum of Dr. Leary himself. Where else but on the Web could you admire the view from Timothy Leary's patio? Well, from Timothy Leary's actual patio, that's where. Trick question.

Ever the innovator, when Dr. Leary found out he had inoperable prostate cancer, he decided to die a very public death on the World Wide Web: he had a "deanimation room" prepared at his home (and home page), where he planned to take his life when he decided it was time. Unfortunately, death beat him to the punch, and he passed away on May 31, 1996.

His admirers have kept the site going as a memorial, however. Visitors can read about Leary's last months: his physical health and state of mind, his thoughts on dying, and his average daily intake of neuroactive drugs, including tobacco, caffeine, alcohol, marijuana, cocaine, speed, prescription drugs, nitrous oxide, psychedelics, and opiates. A handy form is provided in case you want to keep track of your own daily drug intake—just don't take all of them at once, or you may find yourself prematurely deanimated.

Everybody Into the Pool

Yes, yes, so the Web tells you who died and where they're buried. But of what *practical* value is such knowledge? How is that news we can use?

Well, a bunch of sick, sick puppies out there in Web Land have managed to design a contest where the judges' decision is most definitely final: they're called **Death Pools.** You submit a list of the names of ten famous people you think are likely to croak in the next 12 months; the player with the most correct guesses at year's end wins the pot of money. There are several of these morbid "Olympics" being played at this very moment, at sites such as http://www.crl.com/~rfboggs/ace8/aceeight.html, or http://www. personal.u-net.com/~theopera/, or http://www.ftech.net/~sugarman/deadpool.html.

Here are some sample rules from various pools:

- "Each celebrity counts as one point. Amputations do not contribute towards the total."
- "FIVE bonus points if the stiff is 35 years old or under, and a further FIVE bonus points for unexpected checkout: Murder, Suicide, Air Crashes, Car Crashes, etc."
- "Celebs who have been diagnosed terminally ill before the date you send in your entry will not be accepted."

✲ "To get a confirmed kill, news of your player's death must appear in at least two national publications (e.g., the Washington Post, New York Times, Wall Street Journal, or (yikes) even USA Today)."

✲ "Persons currently on Death Row cannot be entered."

✲ "You may not list another Death Pool player on your list (sure, we're friends, but there *is* money involved)."

At some of these sites, you even get a running play-by-play of the most popular nominees for corpsehood. Actual excerpt: "Showing strong in first place it's The Queen Mother. She's 92, or is it 95?, but the punters think it's about time she went. But who's this creeping up in second? It's Ronnie Alzheimer. Now *there's* a name we won't forget."

We hasten to add that we get *absolutely* no amusement out of this depraved little game. None. You'd have to be an absolute sicko to derive any kind of mirth from such a twisted sport.

Except possibly for Rule 15. It describes what happens in the case of a tie. "In the event that two or more players are tied at the end of the year, those players will enter a 'sudden death' period." Get it? *Sudden death?* Oh, man, we could just die laughing.

Facing Your Mortality

So, you thought Death Pools were amusing, eh? Well, **The Death Clock** (http://www.speedoflight.com/techs/ray/death) will sober you up real fast. Enter your birth date and your sex, and this site calculates how long you have left to live, statistically speaking. The Death Clock presents an animated display, counting down the seconds you have left. Tick, tick, tick. . . . Watch it for a few minutes, ruminate on your mortality, and think of all the things you should be doing while the seconds slip inexorably away. Tick, tick, tick. . . . Think of how many of those precious seconds you've frittered away at meaningless activities such as popping virtual bubble wrap (see Chapter 3 of this book), building a virtual Mr. Potato Head (see Chapter 3 of this book), or seeing Chapter 3 of this book. Tick, tick, tick. . . . Then go out there and do something worthwhile, damn it!

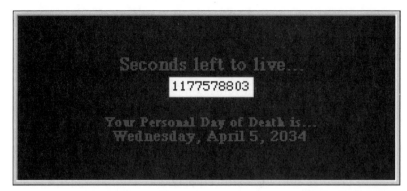

Time's running out ...

Of course, The Death Clock assumes you'll die of natural causes. What if you're murdered next week? It could happen. "Crime exists. Your vulnerability cannot be ignored. Threat assessment is a means for you to calmly evaluate your risks." The **Rate Your Risk** page (http://www.Nashville. Net/~police/risk/), brought to you by the Metropolitan Nashville Police Department, lets you evaluate—calmly or otherwise—your chances of being raped, robbed, stabbed, shot, beaten, murdered, or having your home burglarized.

We took the "Are you going to be murdered?" test, which evaluates various demographic and lifestyle factors (Do you live in a big city?, Do you keep loaded firearms in the house?, Have you recently fired an employee?, and so on). The results were not rosy. We were at moderate risk. "It would be advisable to alter your schedule and traveling techniques. Cut down your public exposure." (Um, you know the names on the cover of this book? They're not our real names; we just made them up. And we're not getting big royalty payments. And even if we did, we wouldn't keep them in cash in our dresser drawers.) Worse yet, we were only a few points below the "dangerous" category, which means we'd be "either an upper class target or suffer from a wanton lifestyle." Hey, who's suffering?

If your Rate Your Risk test results aren't promising, you'll want to start preparing for the inevitable. Your coffin, for example. Why should your bereaved family members spend thousands of dollars for your casket when you can build your own for under $300? Just send $19.50 to Richard Johnstone at the **Carpenter Homemade Casket Plans** site (http://www. volcano.net/~johnstone/caskhome.html), and you'll receive eight pages of detailed casket-building instructions, including a purchase list and drawings. As a bonus, Mr. Johnstone's plans provide simple modifications that turn your homemade coffin into a fully functional piece of furniture (that's before you occupy it, mind you)—a bookcase, armoire, hope chest, or coffee table. We admire the fellow's ingenuity, although we're not sure it's an appropriate design for a hope chest.

Stalling the Reaper

Sure, you have to die. But you don't have to stay dead. At least that's what the folks at **Alcor** (http://www.alcor.org) are betting on. This company gives a more positive meaning to the expression "big chill" by employing the science of *cryonics*, whereby a person's body is frozen after death and stored in a vat of liquid nitrogen. For $120,000 you can purchase a whole-body suspension; those on a budget may wish to opt for the $50,000 neuro-suspension (they freeze your head). The hope, of course, is that "medical science will be able to revive that person in the future, when life extension and anti-aging have become a reality." Personally, we'd opt for the full $120,000 deluxe platter — how'd you like to be awakened in the year 2599 and discover that you're just a head?

How can you be sure that Alcor employees will be around in a few hundred years to thaw you out? Their online brochure assures you that they're in this for the long term; many Alcor employees plan to be frozen, so it's in their best interest to make sure somebody's around to revive them. We think cryonics is a wonderful idea, but we want some sort of written guarantee that if William "Captain Kirk" Shatner—or even his head—is revived at the same time we are (see Chapter 2), he promises not to sing.

The Lighter Side of Death

"Part of you thinks it's in poor taste . . . part of you wants an Extra-Large." So begins "Skeletons in the Closet," the **L.A. County Coroner's Office Gift Shop Unofficial Web Page** (http://www.lacoroner.com). Here's your one-stop shopping destination for morbid items such as the Black Mariah coin bank, a coroner's toe-tag keychain, and—our favorite—beach towels sporting a chalk outline of a body. Plenty of T-shirts, sweatshirts, and other drop-dead fashions are also available via this online catalog. Just the place to find a gift for that special someone.

Hit the beach with these lovely towels from
the L.A. County Coroner's Office Gift Shop.
All logos and designs trademark 1995, 1996 Los Angeles
Department of Coroner, Skeletons in the Closet.

Index